On
Human
Nature

On Human Nature

ROGER SCRUTON

PRINCETON UNIVERSITY PRESS
PRINCETON AND OXFORD

Copyright © 2017 by Princeton University Press
Published by Princeton University Press, 41 William Street,
Princeton, New Jersey 08540
In the United Kingdom: Princeton University Press, 6 Oxford Street,
Woodstock, Oxfordshire OX20 1TR

press.princeton.edu

Cover design by Michael Boland for thebolanddesignco.com

First paperback printing, 2019
Library of Congress Control Number 2016957094
Paper ISBN 9780691183039
Cloth ISBN 978-0-691-16875-3

British Library Cataloging-in-Publication Data is available

This book has been composed in Garamond Premier Pro

Printed on acid-free paper. ∞

Printed in the United States of America

CONTENTS

~

PREFACE

What follows is a revised version of the three Charles E. Test memorial lectures that I gave, under the auspices of the James Madison Program, at Princeton University in fall 2013. I am very grateful to the program and its director, Robert P. George, for the invitation and for the hospitality shown to me during my visit. And I am especially grateful to the lively audience that a visitor can always expect at Princeton and to the spirit of free inquiry that prevails there. In preparing these lectures for publication I am conscious that they are at best a summary of my views and do not in any way deal with all the difficulties that will occur to the attentive reader. Some of these difficulties I have addressed in *The Soul of the World* and in a fourth chapter here added to the lectures; others must await some later attempt to tackle them or else accompany me to the grave.

Earlier drafts were read by Bob Grant, Alicja Gescinska, and two anonymous readers for Princeton University Press, and from the remarks of all four I have benefited enormously.

Scrutopia, Easter 2016

CHAPTER 1

⁓HUMAN KIND⁓

We human beings are animals, governed by the laws of biology. Our life and death are biological processes, of a kind that we witness in other animals too. We have biological needs and are influenced and constrained by genes with their own reproductive imperative. And this genetic imperative manifests itself in our emotional life, in ways that remind us of the body and its power over us.

For centuries poets and philosophers have told stories about erotic love—Plato leading the way. These stories have endowed the object of love with a value, a mystery, and a metaphysical distinction that seem to place it outside the natural order. And in these stories biology seems hardly to figure, even though they are stories that would make little sense were it not for our condition as reproductive animals, who have established their niche by sexual selection.

We are territorial creatures, just like chimpanzees, wolves, and tigers. We claim our territory and fight for it, and our genes, which require just such an exclusive claim over habitat if their replication is to be guaranteed, depend upon our success. Yet when we fight it is, as a rule, in the name of some high ideal: justice, liberation, national sovereignty, even God Himself. Once again, it seems that we are in the habit of telling ourselves stories that make no reference to the biological realities in which they are rooted.

The most noble of human attributes also have their biological underpinning—or so it seems at least. The self-sacrifice that causes a woman to lay everything aside for her children, the courage that enables human beings to endure the greatest hardships and dangers for the sake of something that they value, even those virtues such as temperance and justice that seem to require us to vanquish our own desires—all these things have seemed to many people to have their counterparts among the lower animals and to demand a single explanation, generalizable across species. Personal affection has been brought within the fold of biology, first by Freud's highly metaphorical and now largely discredited theory of the libido and more recently by the attachment theory of John Bowlby, for whom love, loss, and mourning are to be explained, at least in part, as phylogenetic products of our need for a "secure base."[1] Bowlby was a psychiatrist, acutely aware that human beings do not merely inherit their emotional capacities but also adapt and refine them.

---

[1] John Bowlby, *Attachment and Loss*, vols. 1–3 (New York: Basic Books, 1969–1980); John Bowlby, *A Secure Base* (New York: Routledge, 1988).

Nevertheless, he described love, grief, and mourning as biological processes and argued that "the child's tie to his mother is the human version of behaviour seen commonly in many other species of animal."[2]

By putting that behavior in its ethological context Bowlby was able to give a far more plausible account of our primary attachments than those given by Freud and his immediate successors. Our personal affections, he argued, are to be explained in terms of the function that they perform in our "environment of evolutionary adaptedness," and the explanation will not be couched in terms that make any radical ontological division between us and other mammals. The discovery of the hormone oxytocin, and its effect in predisposing animals of many different species toward affectionate relations with their own kind, has further encouraged the view that attachment can be understood and explained without reference to the stories with which we humans embellish it.

When Darwin and Wallace first hit on the idea of natural selection, the question arose whether our many "higher" characteristics, such as morality, self-consciousness, symbolism, art, and the interpersonal emotions, create such a gap between us and the "lower" animals as to demand explanation of another kind. Wallace at first thought that they did not but later changed his mind, coming to the conclusion that there is a qualitative leap in the order of things,

---

[2] Bowlby, *Attachment and Loss*, vol. 1, p. 183.

setting the higher faculties of human kind in a different category from those features that we share with our evolutionary neighbors. As he put it: "We are endowed with intellectual and moral powers superfluous to evolutionary requirements,"[3] and the existence of these powers could therefore not be explained by natural selection for fitness.

Darwin, however, remained attached to the view that *natura non facit saltus* and in writing *The Descent of Man* tried to show that the differences between humans and other animals, great though they are, can nevertheless be reconciled with the theory of stepwise development.[4] For Darwin the moral sense is continuous with the social instincts of other species.[5] Through the theory of sexual selection, he gave an enhanced account of the resources on which natural selection can draw and made the suggestion, taken up in our own time by Steven Pinker and Geoffrey Miller, that many of the "higher" faculties of man, such as art and music, which seem, on the face of it, to be devoid of any evolutionary function, should be seen as resulting from selection at the sexual level.[6] Darwin went

---

[3] A. R. Wallace, *Natural Selection and Tropical Nature: Essays on Descriptive and Theoretical Biology* (London: Macmillan, 1891). See also A. R. Wallace, *Darwinism: An Exposition of the Theory of Natural Selection with Some of Its Applications* (London: Macmillan, 1889), chapter 15.

[4] Charles Darwin, *The Descent of Man*, vol. 1 (New York: Appleton and Co., 1871).

[5] Ibid., pp. 71–72.

[6] Steven Pinker, *How the Mind Works* (London: Allen Lane, 1997), pp. 522–524; Geoffrey Miller, *The Mating Mind: How Sexual Choice Shaped the Evolution of Human Nature* (New York: Doubleday, 2000).

on to give an account of human emotions in which their expression in the face and gestures is compared with the expression of emotion in other animals: and his purpose in all this was to suggest that the perceived gap between us and our evolutionary cousins is no proof of a separate origin.[7]

GENETICS AND GAMES

This controversy has taken on an entirely different character since R. A. Fisher's pioneering work in population genetics.[8] Problems with which Darwin wrestled throughout his life—the sexual selection of dysfunctional features (the problem of the peacock's tail), for example, or the "altruism" of insects (the problem of the anthill)—are radically transformed when the locus of evolution is seen as the self-replicating gene, rather than the sexually reproducing animal.[9] And as John Maynard Smith and G. R. Price showed in an elegant essay,[10] the new way of looking at natural selection, as governed by the replicating "strategies" of genes, permits the application of game

[7] Charles Darwin, *The Expression of the Emotions in Man and Animals* (New York: Appleton and Co., 1898).

[8] R. A. Fisher, *The Genetical Theory of Natural Selection* (1930), revised ed. (New York: Dover, 1958).

[9] See the lively account in Helen Cronin, *The Ant and the Peacock: Altruism and Sexual Selection, from Darwin to Today* (Cambridge: Cambridge University Press, 1991).

[10] J. Maynard Smith and G. R. Price, "The Logic of Animal Conflict," *Nature* 246 (1973): pp. 15–18.

theory to genetic competition, which in turn delivers a neat solution to another famous problem—that of aggression, noticed by Darwin and spelled out in detail by Lorenz.[11] The rut among stags can be derived as an "evolutionarily stable strategy": one that enables the genes of rutting stags to reproduce themselves while providing the genes of hinds with the best return for their reproductive investment. This approach, generalized by R. Axelrod,[12] has had profound consequences, for example, in showing that there might be an evolutionary advantage in reciprocally altruistic cooperation, even when not part of kin selection (as when female bats allegedly share their booty of blood with other unsuccessful females in a colony). It has also suggested a general theory of "altruism," held by its supporters to explain not only the inflexible self-sacrifice of the soldier ant but also the fear-filled and heroic self-sacrifice of the human soldier.[13] In short, we seem to have been brought a step nearer the proof of Darwin's contention that the moral sense is continuous with the social instincts of other species.

[11] Konrad Lorenz, *On Aggression*, trans. Marjorie Kerr Wilson (New York: Harcourt Brace, 1966).

[12] R. Axelrod, *The Evolution of Cooperation* (New York: Basic Books, 1984).

[13] See, for example, Matt Ridley, *The Origins of Virtue: Human Instincts and the Evolution of Cooperation* (London: Viking, 1991). It is important to recognize that the game-theoretic approach to altruism is distinct from the theory of "inclusive fitness," defended in W. D. Hamilton, "The Genetical Evolution of Social Behaviour," *Journal of Theoretical Biology* 7 (1964): pp. 1–16, according to which altruism extends to kin and in proportion to the degree of kinship.

The genetic approach has not been without its critics. Advocates of "group selection" have argued that selection must occur at higher levels than that of the gene if we are to account for such socially complex behavior as the self-limitation of populations and the dispersal patterns of herds.[14] Others have been skeptical of the assumption that there can be small-scale transitions that lead by a chain of changes from the social behavior of animals to the social behavior of people. In particular, Chomsky has argued that the acquisition of language is an all-or-nothing affair, which involves acquiring a rule-guided and creative capacity that cannot be built up from singular connections between words and things.[15] A Chomskian would be dismissive of those attempts to inflict language on animals—on chimpanzees and dolphins, for example—that were once greeted with such enthusiasm, as the proof that they are like us or we are like them.[16] Whatever the

[14]V. C. Wynne-Edwards, *Animal Dispersion in Relation to Social Behaviour* (Edinburgh: Oliver and Boyd, 1962). The original inspiration here is Lorenz, *On Aggression*. Wynne-Edwards is somewhat cantankerously criticized by Richard Dawkins in *The Selfish Gene* (1976), revised ed. (New York: Oxford University Press, 1989), pp. 7–10.

[15]See especially Noam Chomsky, *Language and Mind* (1968), 3rd ed. (Cambridge: Cambridge University Press, 2006), in which language is described as "an example of true emergence—the appearance of a qualitatively different phenomenon at a specific stage of complexity of organization" (p. 62).

[16]For the attempts, see Eugene Linden, *Apes, Men and Language* (New York: Saturday Review Press, 1974); for the enthusiasm, see Mary Midgley, *Beast and Man: The Roots of Human Nature* (London: Routledge, 1978), pp. 215–251.

interest of the word-thing/word-experience connections that animals can make, these are connections of a radically different kind than those embedded in a transformational grammar. They are piecemeal associations that, detached from generative rules and semantic organization, remain no more vehicles of thought, dialogue, and interrogation than the warning cries of birds and bonobos or the wagging tails of dogs. Again, the objection is not widely regarded as conclusive, and geneticists have advanced theories of "protolanguage" that attempt to show both that there could be piecemeal advances toward linguistic competence and that these advances would be selected at the genetic level.[17]

GENES AND MEMES

We know that the human species has adapted to its environment; but we also know that it has adapted its environment to itself. It has passed adaptations to its offspring not only genetically but also culturally. It has shaped its world through information, language, and rational exchange. And while all those features can be acknowledged by biology and given a place in evolutionary theory,[18] that theory will not,

[17] See, for example, John Maynard Smith and Eörs Szathmáry, *The Major Transitions in Evolution* (Oxford: W. H. Freeman, 1995), pp. 303–308.

[18] As exemplified, for instance, by Kim Sterelny, in his theory of cumulative niche construction. See his *Thought in a Hostile World: The Evolution of Human Cognition* (Oxford: Blackwell, 2003).

in the first instance, concern the replication of genes but, rather, the reproduction of societies. Moreover, human societies are not just groups of cooperating primates: they are communities of persons, who live in mutual judgment, organizing their world in terms of moral concepts that arguably have no place in the thoughts of chimpanzees. It is possible that cognitive science will one day incorporate these moral concepts into a theory of the brain and its functions and that theory will be a biological theory. But its truth will be tested against the distinctively human capacities that, according to Wallace, seem "superfluous to evolutionary requirements," and not against the features of our biological makeup that we share with other animals.

Now, philosophers who argue in that way find themselves confronting a powerful current of opinion that has flowed through all the channels of intellectual life since the publication of Richard Dawkins's *The Selfish Gene*. Natural selection can account for all the difficult facts presented by human culture, Dawkins suggests, once we see culture as developing according to the same principles as the individual organism. Just as the human organism is "a survival machine" developed by self-replicating genes, so is a culture a machine developed by self-replicating "memes"—mental entities that use the energies of human brains to multiply, in the way that viruses use the energies of cells. Like genes, memes need *Lebensraum*, and their success depends upon finding the ecological niche that enables them to generate more examples of their kind. That niche is the human brain.[19]

A meme is a self-replicating cultural entity that, lodging in the brain of a human being, uses that brain to reproduce itself—in the way that a catchy tune reproduces itself in hums and whistles, so spreading like an epidemic through a human community, as did "La donna è mobile" the morning after the first performance of *Rigoletto*. Dawkins argues that ideas, beliefs, and attitudes are the conscious forms taken by self-replicating entities, which propagate themselves as diseases propagate themselves, by using the energies of their hosts: "Just as genes propagate themselves in the gene pool by leaping from body to body via sperms or eggs, so memes propagate themselves in the meme pool by leaping from brain to brain via a process which, in the broad sense, can be called imitation."[20] Dennett adds that this process is not necessarily harmful:[21] there are, among parasitic organisms, both symbionts, which coexist harmlessly with their hosts, and mutualists, which positively amplify the host's ability to survive and flourish in its environment.

[19] For various attempts to give a memetic theory of culture, see Robert Aunger, ed., *Darwinizing Culture: The Status of Memetics as a Science* (Cambridge: Cambridge University Press, 2000). The theory of the meme is dismissively criticized by David Stove in "Genetic Calvinism, or Demons and Dawkins," in *Darwinian Fairytales: Selfish Genes, Errors of Heredity, and Other Fables of Evolution* (New York: Encounter Books, 2006), pp. 172–197.

[20] Dawkins, *Selfish Gene*.

[21] Daniel C. Dennett, *Breaking the Spell* (London: Allen Lane, 2006).

To make the theory remotely plausible we must distinguish memes that belong to science from memes that are merely "cultural." Scientific memes are subject to effective policing by the brain that harbors them, which accepts ideas and theories only as part of its own truth-directed method. Merely cultural memes are outside the purview of scientific inference and can run riot, causing all kinds of cognitive and emotional disorders. They are subject to no external discipline, such as that contained in the concept of truth, but follow their own reproductive path, indifferent to the aims of the organism that they have invaded.

That idea is appealing at the level of metaphor, but what does it amount to in fact? From the point of view of memetics, absurd ideas have the same start in life as true theories, and assent is a retrospective honor bestowed on reproductive success. The only significant distinction to be made when accounting for this success is between memes that enhance the life of their hosts and memes that either destroy that life or coexist symbiotically with it. It is one of the distinguishing characteristics of human beings, however, that they can distinguish an idea from the reality represented in it, can entertain propositions from which they withhold their assent, and can move judge-like in the realm of ideas, calling each before the bar of rational argument, accepting them and rejecting them regardless of the reproductive cost.

It is not only in science that this attitude of critical reflection is maintained. Matthew Arnold famously described culture as "a pursuit of our total perfection by means of getting to know, on all matters which most concern us, the best which has been thought and said in the world, and, through this knowledge, turning a stream of fresh and free thought upon our stock notions and habits."[22] Like so many people wedded to the nineteenth-century view of science, Dawkins overlooks the nineteenth-century reaction—which said, "Wait a minute: science is not the only way to pursue knowledge. There is moral knowledge too, which is the province of practical reason; there is emotional knowledge, which is the province of art, literature, and music. And just possibly there is transcendental knowledge, which is the province of religion. Why privilege science, just because it sets out to *explain* the world? Why not give weight to the disciplines that *interpret* the world and so help us to be at home in it?"

That reaction has lost none of its appeal. And it points to a fundamental weakness in "memetics." Even if there are units of memetic information, propagated from brain to brain by some replicating process, it is not they that come before the mind in conscious thinking. Memes stand to ideas as genes stand to organisms: if they exist at all (and no evidence has been given by Dawkins or anyone else for thinking that they do), then their sempiternal and purposeless reproduction is no concern of ours. Ideas, by contrast, form part

---

[22] Matthew Arnold, *Culture and Anarchy: An Essay in Political and Social Criticism* (London, 1869).

of the conscious network of critical thinking. We assess them for their truth, their validity, their moral propriety, their elegance, completeness, and charm. We take them up and discard them, sometimes in the course of our search for truth and explanation, sometimes in our search for meaning and value. And both activities are essential to us. Although culture isn't science, it is nevertheless a conscious activity of the critical mind. Culture—both the high culture of art and music and the wider culture embodied in a moral and religious tradition—sorts ideas by their intrinsic qualities, helps us to feel at home in the world and to resonate to its personal significance. The theory of the meme neither denies that truth nor undermines the nineteenth-century view that culture, understood in that way, is as much an activity of the rational mind as science.

SCIENCE AND SUBVERSION

The concept of the meme belongs with other subversive concepts—Marx's "ideology," Freud's unconscious, Foucault's "discourse"—in being aimed at discrediting common prejudice. It seeks to expose illusions and to explain away our dreams. But it is itself a dream: a piece of ideology, accepted not for its truth but for the illusory power that it confers on the one who conjures with it. It has produced some striking arguments—not least those given by Daniel Dennett in *Breaking the Spell*. But it possesses the very fault for which it purports to be a remedy: it is a spell, with which the scientist mind seeks to conjure away the things that pose a threat to it.

Reflecting on this, it seems clear to me that Wallace had a point in the emphasis that he put on the features that seem to place humanity in a world apart, though he was surely wrong to think of those features as "surplus to evolutionary requirements," for if any of our attributes is adaptive, rationality surely is. But then, rationality is, in one sense of that difficult expression, "of our essence." Wallace was therefore pointing to the fact that we human beings, even if we are animals, belong to a kind that does not occupy a place in the scheme of things comparable to that of the other animals. And the *philosophical* controversy here—a controversy adjacent to that among biologists and evolutionary psychologists concerning the significance of culture—is precisely a controversy about human nature: To what kind do we belong?

Dawkins sets out to explain goals and rational choices in terms of genetic materials that make no choices. He describes these materials as "selfish" entities, motivated by a reproductive "goal," but (at least in his less rhetorical moments) he recognizes that genes are not, and cannot be, selfish, since selfishness is a feature of people, to be characterized in terms of their dispositions and their rational projects.[23] In a cogent

[23] Though David Stove takes Dawkins to task for his constant reference to "selfishness" and his failure to say what it could possibly mean in this context: see Stove, "Genetic Calvinism."

biological theory all such teleological idioms must be replaced with functional explanations.[24] And that is what the recourse to game theory and similar devices is supposed to authorize. A player wants to win and therefore adopts a winning strategy: that is a teleological explanation of this behavior. Natural selection tells us that winning strategies will be selected, even when they describe the behavior of genes that want nothing at all. That is a functional explanation, which says nothing about intentions, choices, or goals.

Functional explanations have a central place in biology.[25] The fact that birds have wings is explained by the function of wings, in enabling birds to fly. The process of random mutation at a certain point produces a winged creature: and in the competition for scarce resources, this creature has the decisive advantage over its rivals. Note, however, that this reference to function only amounts to a causal explanation because it is supplemented by the theory of random mutation—a theory that tells us *how* the existence of a trait is caused by its function. This point bears heavily on the "explanations" of altruism and morality

[24]How teleological thinking can be replaced by functional explanation is one theme of Richard Dawkins's subsequent book, *The Blind Watchmaker* (Oxford: Oxford University Press, 1986). For an illuminating discussion of functional explanations and their application outside biology, see G. A. Cohen, *Karl Marx's Theory of History: A Defence* (Princeton: Princeton University Press, 1978).

[25]See Ron Amundson and George V. Lauder, "Function without Purpose: The Use of Causal Role Function in Evolutionary Biology," in D. Hull and M. Ruse, eds., *The Philosophy of Biology*, Oxford Readings in Philosophy (Oxford: Oxford University Press, 1998), pp. 227–257.

advanced by Axelrod and Maynard Smith. A population genetically averse to cooperation, to parental affection, to self-sacrifice on behalf of children, and to sexual restraint and the control of violence is a population endowed with traits that are dysfunctional relative to reproduction. Hence it will disappear. From this trivial truth, however, we can deduce nothing about the causes of moral conduct or moral thought and nothing about their grounds. It does not follow that morality is the result of natural selection rather than group selection within the species; nor does it follow that morality originates in our biological makeup rather than in the workings of rational thought. In fact nothing follows that would serve either to bypass or to undermine the work of philosophy in exploring the foundations of moral judgment and its place in the life of a rational being.

It is a trivial truth that dysfunctional attributes disappear; it is a substantial theoretical claim that functional attributes exist *because of* their function.[26] And until the theory is produced, the claim is without intellectual weight. You may think that genetics provides the needed theory: for it implies that altruism is the "evolutionally stable" solution to genetic competition within our species. But that explanation only gives a *sufficient* condition for "altruism," and only by

[26] A similar objection can be mounted, it seems to me, against the defense of Marx's theory of history presented by G. A. Cohen (*Karl Marx's Theory of History*). That dysfunctional institutions disappear is no ground for thinking that the existence of an institution is caused by its function.

redescribing altruism in terms that bypass the higher realms of moral thought. If Kant is right about the categorical imperative, then there is an independent sufficient condition, namely, rationality, that tells us to act on that maxim that we can will as a universal law.

Moreover, practical reason explains not only altruism, in the minimalist description favored by geneticists, but also the superstructure of moral thought and emotion. It also suggests a theory of *the kind to which we belong*, and it is a theory at odds with that suggested by the game-theoretic account of genetic self-sacrifice. According to Kant, the kind to which we belong is that of *person*, and persons are by nature free, self-conscious, rational agents, obedient to reason and bound by the moral law. According to the theory of the selfish gene, the kind to which we belong is that of *human animal*, and humans are by nature complicated by-products of their DNA. Kant saw his theory as raising the human being "infinitely above all the other beings on earth."[27] But it is also true that his theory allows that nonhuman beings may nevertheless belong to the same kind as us: angels, for instance, and maybe dolphins too. The selfish gene theory would dismiss the suggestion as nonsense.

In the hands of their popularizers, the biological sciences are used to reduce the human condition

[27] Immanuel Kant, *Anthropology from a Pragmatic Point of View*, ed. Robert Louden and Manfred Kuehn (Cambridge: Cambridge University Press, 2006), p. 1.

to some simpler archetype, on the assumption that what we are is what once we were and that the truth about mankind is contained in our genealogy. The previous wave of pop genetics, which called itself "sociobiology," came up with deliberately disturbing conclusions, such as this one: "Morality has no other demonstrable ultimate purpose than to keep human genetic material intact."[28] Such conclusions depend upon using the language of common sense while at the same time canceling the presuppositions on which commonsense terms depend for their meaning. This trick can be played in almost any area of human thinking and is never more effective than when it is used to pour scorn on our moral and religious ideas. Ordinary people are in the unfortunate position of believing things that are true but which they cannot defend by any rational argument that will withstand the force of scientific reasoning, however flawed that reasoning may be. Hence, by targeting ordinary beliefs—beliefs that, if backed up at all, are backed up by religious faith and not by scientific argument—scientists score easy points and conceal the weakness of their case.[29]

[28] E. O. Wilson, *On Human Nature* (Cambridge, Mass.: Harvard University Press, 1978), p. 168.

[29] This accusation was strongly made against Dawkins, in the context of the original TV series of *The Selfish Gene*, by Mary Midgley (*Beast and Man*, pp. 102–103). Whether Midgley's objections are fair is a moot point; but she deserves credit for recognizing that the challenge presented by Dawkins goes to the heart of philosophical anthropology. Her criticisms of sociobiological writers are more pertinent and have been amplified in her *Evolution as a Religion*, revised ed. (London: Routledge, 2002).

UNDERSTANDING LAUGHTER

I do not deny that we are animals; nor do I dissent from the theological doctrine that our biological functions are an integral part of our nature as human persons and also the objects of fundamental moral choices.[30] But I want to take seriously the suggestion that we must be understood through another order of explanation than that offered by genetics and that we belong to a kind that is not defined by the biological organization of its members. The "selfish gene" theory may be a good account of the origin of the human being: but what a thing is and how it came to be are two different questions, and the answer to the second may not be an answer to the first. It may be as impossible to understand the human person by exploring the evolution of the human animal as it is to discover the significance of a Beethoven symphony by tracing the process of its composition.

Consider one of those features of people that set them apart from other species: laughter. No other animal laughs. What we call the laughter of the hyena is a species sound that happens to resemble human laughter. To be real laughter it would have to be an expression of amusement—laughter *at* something, founded in a complex pattern of thought. True, there is also "laughter at what ceases to amuse," as Eliot puts it. But

[30] This view is eloquently defended by Pope John Paul II in the encyclical *Veritatis Splendor*, August 6, 1993, sections 47 et seq.

we understand this "hollow" laughter as a deviation from the central case, which is the case of amusement. But what is amusement? No philosopher, it seems to me, has ever quite put a finger on it. Hobbes's description of laughter as "sudden glory" has a certain magical quality; but "glory" suggests that all laughter is a form of triumph, which is surely far from the truth. Schopenhauer, Bergson, and Freud have attempted to identify the peculiar thought that lies at the heart of laughter: none, I think, with more than partial success.[31] Helmuth Plessner has seen laughing and crying as keys to the human condition, features that typify our distinctiveness.[32] But his phenomenological language is opaque and leads to no clear analysis of either laughter or tears.

One contention, however, might reasonably be advanced, which is that laughter expresses an ability to accept our all-too-human inadequacies: by laughing we may attract the community of sentiment that inoculates us against despair. This fact about laughter—that it points to a community of sentiment—has been well brought out by Frank Buckley.[33] From that suggestion, however, another follows. Only a being who makes judgments can laugh. Typically we laugh at

[31] See R. Scruton, "Laughter," in *The Aesthetic Understanding* (London: Methuen, 1982), pp. 180–194.

[32] Helmuth Plessner, *Laughing and Crying: A Study in the Limits of Human Behavior*, trans. J. Spencer Churchill and Marjorie Grene (Evanston: Northwestern University Press, 1970).

[33] F. H. Buckley, *The Morality of Laughter* (Ann Arbor: University of Michigan Press, 2003).

things that *fall short* or at witticisms that place our
actions side by side with the aspirations that they
ridicule. If the laughter of children seems not to
conform to that suggestion, it is largely because the
judgments of children, like the laughter that springs
from them, are embryonic—stages on the way to
that full readiness of social assessment that is the
basis of adult life. Insofar as children are amused by
things, it is because, in their own way, they are com-
paring those things with the norms that they challenge. Putative cases of amusement in chimpanzees
should, it seems to me, be understood in a similar
way.[34] Creatures coaxed by their human masters to
the verge of judgment are on the verge of amusement
too. And by getting to the verge they reveal how
wide for them is the chasm that human children will
cross with a single stride.

To explain laughter, therefore, we should have to
explain the peculiar thought processes involved in
our judgments of others; we should have to explain
the pleasure that we feel when ideal and reality conflict and also the peculiar social intentionality of this
pleasure. Of course, we can make a stab at this kind
of explanation, postulating cognitive programs in the
human brain and the biological "wetware" in which
they are imprinted. But as yet the explanation will be a
pure speculation, with little or no input from genetics.

---

[34]For an example, see the case of Roger and Lucy—two chimpanzees
with some competence in the "Ameslan" sign language—described in Linden, *Apes, Men and Language*, p. 97.

I envisage evolutionary psychologists offering the following account of laughter. By laughing together at our faults, they might say, we come to accept them, and this makes cooperation with our imperfect neighbors easier, since it neutralizes anger at our shared inadequacies. Hence a community of laughing people has a competitive advantage over a community of the humorless. A moment's reflection will reveal the emptiness of that explanation. For it assumes what it needs to explain, namely, that laughter promotes cooperation. Admittedly my way of describing laughter suggests that this is so. But it suggests it by quite another route than that presented by biology or the theory of genetics.

I was describing a thought process, involving concepts such as those of fault and ideal that can have no clear place in evolutionary biology, as we now know it. I was assuming that laughter is an expression of understanding and that this understanding may be shared. And at no point did I assume that the sharing of laughter benefits anybody's genes in any of the ways that feature in the theory of genetics. Indeed, so far as my account was concerned, laughter might be an entirely redundant by-product of human life. It seems otherwise only because of my account, which is not a scientific account at all but an exercise in what Dilthey called *Verstehen*— the understanding of human action in terms of its social meaning rather than its biological cause.[35]

---

[35] See Rudolf Makkreel, *Dilthey: Philosopher of the Human Studies* (Princeton: Princeton University Press, 1993). Makkreel is currently

Suppose a group of zoologists were to come across a species that sat around in groups, pointing and emitting laughter-like sounds. How would they set about explaining this behavior? They would *first* have to know whether what they observed was real laughter. In other words they would have to know whether these creatures were laughing *at* something and pointing *at* something. And this word *at* does not yield easily to scientific analysis. It is a marker of intentionality, the "mental direction upon an object," as Brentano described it,[36] and can be deciphered only if we are able to interpret the thought processes from which the behavior in question flows. All the work of explanation, therefore, depends upon a prior work of interpretation, the point of which is to settle the question whether these creatures are like us in being amused by things or whether, on the contrary, they are not like us at all, and their laughter-like behavior is something to be explained in another way. If we come to this second conclusion, the apparatus of ethology can indeed be imported into the case: we can begin to ask what function this laughter-like behavior might perform in securing an ecological niche for the genes of those who engage in it. If we come to the first con-clusion, then we need to understand these creatures as we understand one another—in terms of the way they

editing an accurate and scholarly English edition of Dilthey's works, which is in the course of publication by Princeton University Press.

[36] Franz Brentano, *Psychology from an Empirical Standpoint*, trans. L. McAlister (London: Routledge, 1974), p. 77.

conceptualize the world and the values that motivate their response to it.

I used the phrase "like us," implying that amusement is one of our characteristics. And the question before us is how we should unpack that phrase. What do we mean when we refer to "creatures like us"? Do we mean to include only humans? Or do we have some wider, or perhaps narrower, category in mind? Homer tells us of the "laughter of the gods," and Milton of laughter among the angels. Here is the beginning of a profound metaphysical problem. We belong to a natural kind, the kind *Homo sapiens sapiens*, which is a biological species. But when we talk of creatures like us, it seems that we do not necessarily refer to our species membership.

One last point about laughter. As I described it laughter seems to have a beneficial effect on human communities: those who laugh together also grow together and win through their laughter a mutual toleration of their all-too-human defects. But not everything that confers a benefit has a function. Entirely redundant behavior—jumping for joy, listening to music, bird-watching, prayer—may yet confer enormous benefits. By calling it redundant I mean that those benefits are the effect of the behavior, not its cause. That is how it is with laughter. There are communities of the humorless in which laughter is perceived as a threat and severely punished. But the humorless community is not for that reason dysfunctional; in itself it is as well equipped for survival as a community of comedians.

It is arguable indeed that the humorless Puritanism of the Massachusetts colonists was an important stimulus to their survival strategies during the early years. But the thing that they lacked would nevertheless have been a benefit to them, since laughter is something that rational beings enjoy.

THE GENEALOGY OF BLAME

I turn now to another feature of the human condition that divides us from our simian relatives: the feature of responsibility. We hold each other accountable for what we do, and as a result we understand the world in ways that have no parallel in the lives of other species. Our world, unlike the environment of an animal, contains rights, deserts, and duties; it is a world of self-conscious subjects, in which events are divided into the free and the unfree, those that have reasons and those that are merely caused, those that stem from a rational subject and those that erupt into the stream of objects with no conscious design. Thinking of the world in this way, we respond to it with emotions that lie beyond the repertoire of other animals: indignation, resentment, and envy; admiration, commitment, and praise—all of which involve the thought of others as accountable subjects, with rights and duties and a self-conscious vision of their future and their past. Only responsible beings can feel these emotions, and in feeling them, they situate themselves in some way outside the natural order, standing back from it in judgment. From Plato to Sartre, philosophers have differed radically in their attempts to account for these peculiar features of the human condition: but almost all have agreed in searching for a philosophical rather than a scientific account.

There is one interesting historical exception to that claim, however, and that is Nietzsche, who, in *The Genealogy of Morals*, tries to explain the origins of responsibility in a way that anticipates the more recent attempts of geneticists to account for the moral life in terms of survival strategies that benefit our genes. Nietzsche envisages a primeval human society, reduced to near-universal slavery by the "beasts of prey," as he calls them—namely, the strong, self-affirming, healthy egoists who impose their desires on others by the force of their nature. The master race maintains its position by punishing all deviation on the part of the slaves—just as we punish a disobedient horse. The slaves, too timid and demoralized to rebel, receive this punishment as a retribution. Because they cannot exact revenge, the slaves expend their resentment on themselves, coming to think of their condition as in some way deserved, a just recompense for their inner transgressions. Thus is born the sense of guilt and the idea of sin. From the *ressentiment*, as he calls it, of the slave, Nietzsche goes on to derive an explanation of the entire theological and moral vision of Christianity.

According to Nietzsche's genealogy, the master race benefits from the subjection of the slaves—and you can see this as the premise of a protobiological, even protogenetic, explanation of its social strategy. The master race secures its position by a regime of punishment, and in due course the punishment is internalized by the slave to engender ideas of guilt, blame, desert, and justice. But why should the slave understand punishment in these elaborate and moralized terms? Why should the internalization of punishment lead to *guilt* rather than *fear*? A horse certainly fears the whip: But when has it felt guilty for provoking it? Why is the original exercise of force seen as a *punishment* rather than a mere need on the part of the one who inflicts it?

What, after all, is the distinction between suffering inflicted as a means to securing one's ends and suffering inflicted as a punishment? Surely the difference lies in the mind of the agent. The trainer thinks that the suffering he inflicts is *needed*; the one who punishes thinks that it is *due*. That is due which is deserved, and that is deserved which may be rightly and justly inflicted. In short, punishment is a moral idea, to be unpacked in terms of those concepts of justice, desert, and responsibility that Nietzsche was supposed to be explaining. His genealogy of morals works only because he has read back into the cause all the unexplained features of the effect. In other words, it is not a genealogy at all but a recognition that the human condition, in whatever primitive form you imagine it, is the condition of "creatures like us," who laugh and cry, praise and blame, reward and punish—that is, who live as responsible beings, accountable for their actions.[37]

There are other momentous truths about the human condition that, while often overlooked or downplayed by biologically minded thinkers, occupy a central place in the outlook of ordinary people: for example, there is the fact that we are persons, who regulate our communities through laws ascribing duties and rights. Some philosophers—Aquinas notably but also Locke and Kant—argue that it is "person," not "human being," that is the true name of our kind. And this prompts a metaphysical question brought to the fore by Locke and still disputed, which is that of personal identity. What is the relation between "same person" and "same human being" when both are said of Jill? Which description engages with the fundamental kind under which Jill is individuated and reidentified? I mention that question not so as to suggest an answer to it but in order to highlight the difficulties confronting the view that Jill is in some way reducible to the biological processes that explain her.[38] Under what conditions do those processes reproduce the person who Jill *is*?

[37] Nietzsche's attempted derivation of the moral sense has been undertaken from the standpoint of evolutionary biology by Philip Kitcher, in *The Ethical Project* (Cambridge, Mass.: Harvard University Press, 2011). It is for Kitcher's readers to judge whether he succeeds in explaining the emergence of the moral sense without assuming it.

[38] Moves toward an answer are given in David Wiggins, *Sameness and Substance Renewed* (Cambridge: Cambridge University Press, 2001), chapter 7.

There is also the division that separates merely conscious creatures from *self*-conscious creatures like us. Only the second have a genuine "first-person" perspective, from which to distinguish how things seem to *me* from how they seem to *you*. Creatures with "I" thoughts have an ability to relate to others of their kind that sets them apart from the rest of nature, and many thinkers (Kant, Fichte, and Hegel preeminently) believe that it is this fact, not the fact of consciousness per se, that creates or reveals the central mysteries of the human condition. Although dogs are conscious, they do not reflect on their own consciousness as we do: they live, as Schopenhauer put it, in "a world of perception," their thoughts and desires turned outward to the perceivable world.

I have tried to illustrate the way in which, in order to construct vivid biological explanations of our mental life, we are tempted to read back into the biology all the things that it ought to be trying to explain. To aim for a plausible theory of human nature we must first of all resist that temptation. And we must be prepared to admit that such laws of species-being as we have established—the laws of genetics and the functional account of inherited characteristics—are not yet adequate either to describe or to explain our normal behavior. They fall short of the target, for the very reason that what we are is not the thing that they assume us to be. We are animals certainly; but we are also incarnate persons, with cognitive capacities that are not shared by other animals and which endow us with an entirely distinctive emotional life—one dependent on the self-conscious thought processes that are unique to our kind.

THE EMBODIED PERSON

This returns us to the problem of the relation between the human animal and the person. This problem, as I see it, is not biological but philosophical. I can make only a tentative suggestion in response to it—a suggestion that has something in common with what Aristotle meant when he described the soul as the form of the body and with what Aquinas meant when he argued that, while we are individuated through our bodies, *what* is individuated thereby is not the body but the person.[39] I would suggest that we understand the person as an emergent entity, rooted in the human being but belonging to another order of explanation than that explored by biology.

An analogy might help. When painters apply paint to canvas they create physical objects by purely physical means. Any such object is composed of areas and lines of paint, arranged on a surface that we can regard, for the sake of argument, as two-dimensional. When we look at the surface of the painting, we see those areas and lines of paint and also the surface that contains them. But that is not all we see. We also

[39] Aristotle, *De anima*; Thomas Aquinas, *Summa Theologiae*, 1, 19, 4.

see—for example—a face that looks out at us with smiling eyes. In one sense the face is a property of the canvas, over and above the blobs of paint; for you can observe the blobs and not see the face, and vice versa. And the face is really there: someone who does not see it is not seeing correctly. On the other hand, there is a sense in which the face is not an additional property of the canvas, over and above the lines and blobs. For as soon as the lines and blobs are there, so is the face. Nothing more needs to be added in order to generate the face—and if nothing more needs to be added, the face is surely nothing more. Moreover, every process that produces just these blobs of paint, arranged in just this way, will produce just this face—even if the artist is unaware of the face. (Imagine how you would design a machine for producing Mona Lisas.)

Maybe personhood is an "emergent" feature of the organism in that way: not something over and above the life and behavior in which we observe it but not reducible to them either. Personhood emerges when it is possible to relate to an organism in a new way— the way of personal relations. (In like manner we can relate to a figurative picture in ways that we cannot relate to something that we see merely as a distribution of pigments.) With this new order of relation comes a new order of explanation, in which reasons and meanings, rather than causes, are sought in answer to the question "Why?" With persons we are in dialogue: we call upon them to justify their conduct in our eyes, as we must justify our conduct in theirs. Central to this dialogue are concepts of freedom, choice, and accountability, and these concepts have no place in the description of animal behavior, just as the concept of a human being has no place in the description of the physical makeup of a picture, even though it is a picture in which a human being can be seen.

There is another thought that is helpful in describing the relation between persons and their bodies, a thought first given prominence by Kant and thereafter emphasized by Fichte, Hegel, Schopenhauer, and a whole stream of thinkers down to Heidegger, Sartre, and Thomas Nagel. As a self-conscious subject I have a point of view on the world. The world *seems* a certain way to me, and this "seeming" defines my unique perspective. Every self-conscious being has such a perspective, since that is what it means to be a subject of consciousness. When I give a scientific account of the world, however, I am describing objects only. I am describing the way things are and the causal laws that govern them. This description is given from no particular perspective. It does not contain words such as *here*, *now*, and *I*; and while it is meant to explain the way things seem, it does so by giving a theory of how they are. In short, the subject is in principle unobservable to science, not because it exists in another realm but because it is not part of the empirical world. It lies on the edge of things, like a horizon, and could never be grasped "from the other side," the side of subjectivity itself. Is it a real part of the real world? The question is surely wrongly phrased, since it misconstrues the deep grammar of self-reference and of the reflexive pronoun. When I refer to myself I am not referring to another *object* that is, as it were, hidden in the lining of the observable Roger Scruton. Self-reference is not reference to a Cartesian self but reference to this thing, the thing that I am, namely, an object with a subjective view.

We are not entitled to reify the "self" as a distinct object of reference. Nor can we accept—given the force of Wittgenstein's antiprivate language argument—that our mental states exhibit publicly inaccessible features that somehow define what they really and essentially are.[40] Nevertheless, it is still the case that self-reference radically affects the way in which people relate to one another. Once in place, self-attribution and self-reference become the primary avenues to what we think, intend, and are. They

[40] Though we should note the tenacity of the view that the felt "quale" of a mental state is a *fact* about it, inwardly but not outwardly observable, and bound up with its essential nature. It seems to me that the notion of qualia is an empty hypothesis, a wheel that turns nothing in the mechanism, as Wittgenstein would put it. In an interesting essay, however, Ned Block—one of the most sophisticated defenders of qualia in the current literature—argues that Wittgenstein inadvertently commits himself to the existence of qualia, in a form that goes against the tenor of his philosophy. Ned Block, "Wittgenstein and Qualia," *Philosophical Perspectives* 21, no. 1 (2007): pp. 73–115. The debate here goes so far beyond the scope of these lectures that I can only refer the reader to the brilliant summary by Michael Tye (an equally sophisticated defender of qualia) in the Stanford Encyclopedia of Philosophy: http://plato.stanford.edu /entries/qualia. The position I take can be gleaned from my "The Unobservable Mind," *MIT Technology Review*, February 1, 2005, https://www .technologyreview.com/s/403673/the-unobservable-mind/.

permit us to relate to each other as subjects and not as objects only; and that is what lies at the heart of those ideas for which Nietzsche gave his pseudo-scientific genealogy: ideas of responsibility, account-ability, guilt, praise, and blame. By relating to Jill in this way, I come face-to-face with her: her essential being as a person "emerges" from her bodily reality, in the way that the face emerges from the colored blobs on the canvas.

INTENTIONALITY

In a series of books and essays Daniel Dennett has ar-gued for the view that human beings are "intentional systems"—organisms that exhibit intentional states that are systematically connected.[41] The behavior of intentional systems can be explained or predicted by attributing "propositional attitudes": by describ-ing them as both representing the world and seeking to change it. Not all intentional systems are human: Some animals exhibit intentional states; maybe computers, when sophisticated in the way that Tur-ing foretold, can exhibit them too. Dennett himself takes an easygoing attitude, allowing anything to be an intentional system if our treating it as such gives us some ability to predict its behavior—so that even

---

[41] D. C. Dennett, "Intentional Systems," *Journal of Philosophy* 68 (1971), reprinted in *Brainstorms* (Cambridge, Mass.: MIT Press, 1978).

a thermostat is an intentional system in Dennett's view.[42] His motive in taking this line is to make way for a "genealogy" of intentionality, building toward "aboutness" from simple feedback mechanisms that operate unmysteriously in the ordinary physical world. But it is not necessary to follow Dennett in this. Whatever the genealogy of the intentional, we must recognize the very real difference that exists between behavior that is caused by and expressive of an intentional state and behavior that is not.

Brentano's original insight has been taken by subsequent philosophy to imply that an intentional state is founded on a reference that may fail or a thought that may be false.[43] We can attribute such a state only where there is the possibility of referential failure. Animals exhibit intentionality through their beliefs and desires; they may even exhibit the kind of nonpropositional intentionality in which an object is "before the mind" and mentally targeted—as when a dog barks *at* an intruder, whether or not an intruder is there. It is certainly true that we are intentional systems and that this is a feature of our biological organization. Our brains are not merely devices for mediating between

[42] See, for example, D. C. Dennett, *Kinds of Minds* (London: Weidenfeld, 1996), p. 34.

[43] See the classic essay R. M. Chisholm, "Sentences about Believing," *Proceedings of the Aristotelian Society* 56, no. 1 (1955–1956): pp. 125–148. It is doubtful that this interpretation represents what Brentano really meant, however. See Barry Smith, *Austrian Philosophy* (LaSalle, Ill.: Open Court, 1994).

stimulus and response but instruments that enable us
to think about and perceive the world and which lead
us at times to think about it and perceive it wrongly.

In referring to the emergence of personality and
self-consciousness, however, I am not referring only
to this familiar feature of the human condition. I am
referring, as Dennett has pointed out,[44] to a higher
level of intentionality, one that is only doubtfully exhibited by other animals and which has certainly not
been simulated by a computer.

A dog sees its owner as a living thing, capable of
eye contact; but there is no place in its mental repertoire for the thought of its owner as a "subject of
consciousness," capable also of I-contact. By contrast,
we humans respond to each other and to other animals *as* intentional systems, recognizing a distinction
between how things are in the world and how they
seem to other observers and adopting the "intentional
stance" that Dennett again has emphasized in a series
of books and essays.[45] But once we admit the existence
of the intentional stance—the stance that interprets
the behavior of other creatures in terms of the propositional attitudes expressed in it—we must recognize
a higher (because more conceptually complex) level
of intentionality. Our attitude to a dog is toward a
creature with beliefs and desires; our attitude toward

---

[44] D. C. Dennett, *Consciousness Explained* (London: Allen Lane, 1991).
[45] D. C. Dennett, *The Intentional Stance* (Cambridge, Mass.: MIT Press, 1987).

a normal human being is toward a creature that *attributes* beliefs and desires to itself and to others and therefore to us.

Recognizing that others take this perspective on us, we become accountable for what we think and do, and we try to understand and relate to one another as responsible subjects of consciousness, each of whom has a unique perspective that informs his or her thoughts and actions. By describing this personal perspective as an "emergent" feature of the organism I am offering no theory of its nature—anymore than I am offering a theory of pictures when I say that they emerge from the physical marks in which we see them. Rather, I am saying that at a certain level of complexity, a way of seeing others and ourselves becomes available to us and through this way of seeing we are confronted with another world than that described by evolutionary biology. This other world is the world in which we live—the *Lebenswelt*, to use Husserl's term—the world of interpersonal attitudes.[46]

---

[46] The view I am arguing for has some connection with that defended by P. F. Strawson in "Freedom and Resentment," in his *Freedom and Resentment and Other Essays* (London: Methuen, 1974), pp. 1–28. Unlike Strawson, however, I believe that the human being is truly represented in our interpersonal attitudes and falsely represented in those attitudes Strawson calls "objective." The higher-order intentionality to which I refer—which is the ability to form mental representations of mental representations (one's own and other people's)—has been described, in important psychological studies by Alan Leslie and others, as "metarepresentation." See, e.g., A. Leslie and D. Roth, "What Autism Teaches Us about Metarepresentation," in S. Baron-Cohen, H. Tager Flusberg, and

EMERGENCE AND MATERIALISM

Hard-line reductionists might respond in the following way: emergent properties, they might argue, are nothing "over and above" the physical properties in which we perceive them. The aspect of a picture, for example, emerges automatically when the shapes and colors are laid down on the canvas, and any other production of those same shapes and colors produces just that aspect. The aspect is "a mere appearance," with no reality beyond that of the colored patches in which it is seen. Likewise with personality, which is nothing over and above the biological organization in which we perceive it, since all its features are generated by the biology of the body, and no other input is required.

That response is in fact irrelevant. For the argument concerns what Hegel would call a "transition from quantity to quality." Incremental additions of colored patches to a canvas at a certain point produce a human face: and we are presented with the experience that Wittgenstein describes as "the dawning of an aspect."[47] From this point on we do not merely see the picture differently: we respond to it in another way. We find reasons for the disposition of colored patches that could not have been pertinent before;

D. Cohen, eds., *Understanding Other Minds: Perspectives from Autism* (Oxford: Oxford University Press, 1993).

[47] See Ludwig Wittgenstein, *Philosophical Investigations* (Oxford: Oxford University Press, 1953), part 2, section xi.

and we make a distinction between those who understand the picture and those who do not. The picture takes its place in *another context*, under another order of understanding and another order of explanation than that which pertains to colored patches on a canvas. And that is what happens to an organism when, as the result of whatever incremental steps, it crosses the chasm from the animal to the personal and the aspect of free self-consciousness dawns. Everything in its behavior then appears in a new light. It not only can but must be understood in a new way, through concepts that situate it in the web of personal accountability.

There is an interesting response that might be made to the position I have adopted concerning the emergent nature of the human person—a response that picks up on an argument of Paul Churchland's, in favor of "eliminative materialism."[48] Churchland believes that "folk psychology," in which propositional attitudes play a major role, is a genuine *theory* of human behavior—and one that might turn out to be false. After all, folk psychology accounts for only a small segment of human mentality, containing no theory of memory retrieval, of image construction, of visual-motor coordination, of sleep and a thousand other vital aspects of the mind. Any theory that offered to explain those things, while also matching or outstripping

<hr/>

[48] Paul Churchland, "Eliminative Materialism and the Propositional Attitudes," in W. Lycan, ed., *Mind and Cognition* (Oxford: Basil Blackwell, 1990), pp. 206–221.

the predictive power of our ordinary mental concepts, would replace folk psychology in the same way that relativity theory replaced Newtonian mechanics. We might hold onto folk psychology for simplicity's sake, as we hold onto Newtonian mechanics; but this would not alter the fact that its ontological presuppositions might no longer be tenable. There are brain processes and their information-carrying potential. But maybe the true theory of our behavior makes no reference to beliefs, desires, intentions, and perceptions. Churchland gives reasons for thinking that we might come to this conclusion and that it is in fact the way in which cognitive science is going. Folk psychology might end up as a mere *façon de parler*.

It seems to me that the developments predicted by Churchland would no more rid our world of propositional attitudes than the physical theory of the picture, in terms of the disposition of pigments, rids our world of the painted image. Suppose the true theory of Jill's motive, when she helps me out of sympathy for me, mentions only digital processes in her brain and the muscular response to them. To those brain processes I have no emotional reaction: they could not be targeted by the emotions that I direct toward Jill and are an object at best of scientific curiosity. The intentional object of my own response to her—that toward which I *feel*, *think*, and *intend* on encountering her behavior—must be described in terms of folk psychology. It is only *as so described* that her behavior awakens my emotions. And these in turn are objects for Jill, *only as so described.* Now a third party, observing the relations between us, may be better placed to explain them in neurophysiological terms rather than by attributing propositional attitudes. However, we ourselves are not in the position of that third party. I understand Jill as motivated in just the way that I am motivated, and my own motives are given to me in consciousness only in folk-psychological terms. The pattern of my relations with Jill is built on the supposition that we conceptualize our own and the other's behavior in personal terms. The neurophysiology may give a complete theory of what we so conceptualize, but we could deploy that theory only with the effect of changing our behavior, so that the theory is strictly useless to *us* in understanding and reacting to each other. What we are trying to describe in describing personal relations is revealed *only* on the surface of personal interaction. The personal eludes biology in just the way that the face in the picture eludes the theory of pigments. The personal is not an *addition* to the biological: it emerges *from* it, in something like the way the face emerges from the colored patches on a canvas.

THE PERSON AND THE SUBJECT

There is another, more interesting reason for thinking that the person cannot be eliminated from our account of human nature, which is the interconnectedness between the concept of the person and that of the subject. My reaction to you is dependent on the knowledge that you identify yourself in the first person, just as I do. The practice of giving, receiving, and criticizing reasons for action depends upon the self-attribution of those reasons, and in general all our interpersonal responses are dependent on the belief that others attribute beliefs, attitudes, reasons, and emotions to themselves. I react to you with resentment because you consciously intended to hurt me, and that means that you consciously attributed to yourself just such an intention. I express my resentment with accusations of *you*, which I expect you to meet with a confession or plea phrased in terms of "I." Those who respond to an accusation by describing themselves in the third-person case are either insane or avoiding the issue.

If we are to relate to each other as I to I, then our self-attributions must obey the logic of the first-person case. We must ascribe intentional states to ourselves immediately, on no basis and with first-person privilege, if we are really to identify ourselves as "I" and not as "he" or "she." But this first-person privilege is contained in the logic of folk psychology. It is a feature of the concept of intention that someone knows immediately and on no basis what his or her intentions are. This is not a feature of any of the concepts deployed by brain science: hence brain science could not replace folk psychology in first-person awareness without that awareness ceasing to be a genuine awareness of self. It follows that brain science cannot play the role in interpersonal relations that self-knowledge irreplaceably plays. Were brain science to replace folk psychology, the whole world of interpersonal relations would disintegrate. The concept of the person, and its attendant idea of first-person awareness, is part of the *phenomenon* and not to be eliminated by the science that explains it.

Personality, as I have described it, is an adaptive trait, and all those studies that argue for a cultural input into the evolutionary process can be seen as recognizing this truth.[49] A creature with personality has ways of calling on the help and cooperation of others, ways of influencing them, ways of learning from and teaching them, which are maximally responsive to changes in external circumstances and internal goals. If, by incremental steps, a set of genes can make the "transition from quantity to quality" that has personality as its end point, it has scored an enormous evolutionary advantage. It now has fighting for it, in the sunlit world of rational agency, a knight in armor who has his own compelling reasons for advancing the cause of friends, family, and offspring. He does not need to rely on the strategies implanted in his genes in order to be motivated toward altruism, forgiveness, and the pursuit of virtue: if Kant is right, the

---

[49] For example, Robert Boyd and Peter J. Richerson, *Culture and the Evolutionary Process* (Chicago: University of Chicago Press, 1985); and Sterelny, *Thought in a Hostile World*.

motive toward these things is implicit in the very fact of self-consciousness.[50]

Taking a sober look at the many attempts to describe some part of what is distinctive of the human condition—the use of language (Chomsky, Bennett), second-order desires (Frankfurt), second-order intentions (Grice), convention (Lewis), freedom (Kant, Sartre), self-consciousness (Kant, Fichte, Hegel), laughing and crying (Plessner), the capacity for cultural learning (Tomasello)—you will surely be persuaded that each is tracing some part of a single holistic accomplishment.[51] Now there is nothing in the theory of evolution, either in its original Darwinian form or in the form of Fisherian genetics, that forbids the jump from one mode of explanation and understanding to another. To believe that incremental change is incompatible with radical divides is precisely to misunderstand what Hegel meant by the transition from quantity to quality. There are no intermediate stages between the conscious animal and the

[50] If it were *only* Kant who thought this, then of course there is an opening here for the skeptic. The thought is, however, common from Kant, Fichte, Hegel, and Schopenhauer to Shaftesbury, Smith, Hutcheson, and Hume and to countless contemporary thinkers.

[51] Chomsky, *Language and Mind*; Jonathan Bennett, *Linguistic Behaviour* (Cambridge: Cambridge University Press, 1976); Harry G. Frankfurt, "Freedom of the Will and the Concept of a Person," *Journal of Philosophy* 68, no. 1 (1971): pp. 5–20; H. P. Grice, "Meaning," *Philosophical Review* 66, no. 3 (1957): pp. 377–388, and its many sequels; David Lewis, *Convention: A Philosophical Study* (Cambridge: Cambridge University Press, 1969); Michael Tomasello, *The Cultural Origins of Human Cognition* (Cambridge, Mass.: Harvard University Press, 2000).

self-conscious animal, anymore than there are intermediate stages between patterns in which you cannot see a face and patterns in which you can. Once arrived on the scene, however, the self-conscious creature has an adaptation that will cause it to populate the earth and bend it to its purposes. And, as we know all too well, not all those purposes will be adaptive.

VERSTEHEN AND FAITH

If we now turn back to the question of human nature, we find ourselves equipped to say something about the kind to which we belong. We are the kind of thing that relates to members of its kind through interpersonal attitudes and through the self-predication of its own mental states. Now the intentional states of a creature reflect its conceptual repertoire. To understand your emotions I must know how you conceptualize the world. I cannot simply describe your behavior as though it were a response to the-world-as-science-would-describe-it. There are concepts that direct our mental states but which can play no role in an explanatory theory, because they divide the world into the wrong kinds of kind—concepts such as those of ornament, melody, duty, freedom. The concept of the person is such a concept, which does not mean that there are no persons but, rather, that a scientific theory of persons will classify them with other things—for example, with apes or mammals—and will not be a scientific theory of every kind of person. (For example, it will not be a theory of corporate persons, of angels, or of God.) Hence the kind to which we belong is defined through a concept that does not feature in the science of human biology. That science sees us as objects rather than subjects, and its descriptions of our responses are not descriptions of what we feel. The study of our *kind* is the business of the *Geisteswissenschaften*, which are not sciences at all but "humanities"—in other words, exercises in *Verstehen*, which is the kind of understanding exhibited in my account of laughter.

I have argued that, while we human beings belong to a kind, that kind cannot be characterized merely in biological terms but, rather, only in terms that make essential reference to the web of interpersonal reactions. These reactions bind us to each other and also reach out to (even if they may not connect with) persons who are not of this world and not of the flesh. This thought may produce metaphysical qualms in the reader. After all, how can I be a member of a species while belonging to a kind that is defined not in terms of its biological constitution but in terms of its psychosocial capacities? It is helpful here to turn back to the case of the picture. A picture is a surface that presents to the normal educated eye an aspect of a thing depicted. That is the kind to which pictures belong, and we know that members of this kind include an enormous variety of objects: canvases, sheets of paper, computer screens, holographs, and so on. The behavioral complexity required to exemplify interpersonal responses, to entertain "I"-thoughts, and to hold oneself and others accountable for changes in the world is something that we witness only in members of a particular natural kind—the kind *Homo sapiens sapiens*. But could we not envisage other beings, members of some other species or of no biological species at all, who exhibit the same complexity and are able to engage with us, I to I? If so, they belong with us in the order of things, and there is a kind that includes us both.

Religious people, by holding onto their faith, hold onto that kind of deep, but metaphysically unsettling, truth about the human condition. They have no difficulty in understanding that human beings are distinguished from other animals by their freedom, self-consciousness, and responsibility. And they have a ready supply of stories and doctrines that make sense of those truths. But those truths would be truths even without religion, and it is one task of philosophy in our time to show this. On the other hand, philosophical reasoning often filters through to the lives of ordinary mortals through the channels afforded by doctrine, and one of the problems for the religious believer is that of understanding the precise relation between the conclusions of philosophy and the premises of faith.

The problem here is not a new one. Plato had an inkling of it, and it is Plato's influence that can be discerned in al-Fārābī when he claims that the truths furnished to the intellect by philosophy are made available to the imagination by religious faith.[52]

---

[52] Al-Fārābī, *Fī Taḥsīl as-Saʿādah*, quoted in Lenn E. Goodman, *Islamic Humanism* (Oxford: Oxford University Press, 2003), p. 9.

This thought, developed by Avicenna and Averroës, entered the consciousness of medieval Europe. In the writings of Averroës it borders on the heresy of "double truth": the heresy of believing that reason may justify one thing, and faith, another and incompatible thing. This idea, ascribed to the troublemaker Siger of Brabant, called forth a round condemnation from Aquinas. And it is one that no modern philosopher is likely to find congenial. The point made by al-Fārābī is the more measured one, that truths discoverable to reason may also be revealed—but in another, more imagistic, more metaphorical form—to the eye of faith. Those incapable of reasoning their way to the intricate truths of theology may nevertheless grasp them imaginatively in ritual and prayer, living by a form of knowledge that they lack the intellect to translate into rational arguments.

The work of philosophy that I have sketched stands to be completed by a work of the imagination. For the person with religious faith this work has already been accomplished; for skeptics, however, it must begin anew. The philosophical truth that our kind is not a biological category is swept out of view by scientistic "clairantism" (to use J. L. Austin's felicitous word). It can be conjured back by stories, images, and evocations, in something like the way that Milton conjured the truth of our condition from the raw materials of Genesis. Milton's allegory is not just a portrait of our kind; it is an invitation to kindness. It shows us what we are and what we must live up to. And it sets a standard for art. Take away religion, however, take away philosophy, take away the higher aims of art, and you deprive ordinary people of the ways in which they can represent their apartness. Human nature, once something to live up to, becomes something to live down to instead. Biological reductionism nurtures this "living down," which is why people so readily fall for it. It makes cynicism respectable and degeneracy chic. It abolishes our kind—and with it our kindness.

CHAPTER 2

⌒HUMAN RELATIONS⌒

Ever since Kant, it has been clear that "I" thoughts are fundamental to the life of the person, committing us to the belief in freedom and to the appeal to reason. Just as fundamental, Stephen Darwall has argued, are "you" thoughts—thoughts about the person to whom I am accountable or to whom my reasons are addressed. The moral life depends on something that Darwall calls the "second-person standpoint"—the standpoint of someone whose reasons and conduct are essentially addressed to others.[1] In this chapter I wish to develop that idea.

When I give another person a reason for action, I am assuming that I have the standing, the authority, and the competence to do this. And I also confer standing, authority, and competence on the other. It is not that I draw the other's attention to some reason that exists independently, in the nature of things. The moral dialogue is one in which *I* give reasons to *you*

[1] Stephen Darwall, *The Second-Person Standpoint* (Cambridge, Mass.: Harvard University Press, 2006).

and these reasons have weight for you precisely because that is what I am doing. Suppose you are standing on my foot. There is a reason for you to remove your foot from mine—namely, that this will relieve me of the pain. But there is a reason that I can also give to you that has quite another authority—namely, that I don't want you to stand on my foot. This reason is addressed from me to you, and its force depends upon the shared assumption that you are accountable to me for your voluntary actions insofar as they affect me.

The I-You relation was singled out in a famous book by Martin Buber, a Jewish philosopher and theologian who wrote between the two world wars and whose ideas had a powerful influence in literary circles of the day.[2] What Buber never made clear, however, was that the I-You relation enters essentially into every aspect of the moral life. This is what Darwall has set out to show, arguing that moral norms owe their force ultimately to the second-person reasons that are marshaled by them, that the relations that invite moral judgment and make it possible are relations built upon the second-person standpoint, and that concepts vital to the moral life—such as responsibility, freedom, guilt, and blame—all get their sense, in the end, from the I-You relation in which the giving and receiving of reasons is part of the deal. Adopting and adapting a famous argument of Peter

[2] Martin Buber, *Ich und Du* (1923), English translation, *I and Thou*, trans. Ronald Gregor Smith (New York: Scribner's, 1937).

Strawson's, Darwall shows that emotions such as re-sentment, guilt, gratitude, and anger are not human versions of responses that we might observe in other animals but ways in which the demand for account-ability, which arises spontaneously between creatures who can know themselves as "I," translates into the language of feeling.[3] At the heart of these emotions lies the belief in the freedom of the other, a belief that is irreducible, in that we cannot discard it without ceasing to be what we fundamentally are. For what we are is what we are for each other—relation is built into the very idea of the human person, who is a first person held within the second-person standpoint like a lodestone in a magnetic field.

THE FIRST-PERSON CASE

The moral truth that our obligations are derived from the I-You relation is founded on a metaphysical truth, which is that the self is a social product. It is only be-cause we enter into free relations with others that we can know ourselves in the first person. The arguments for this metaphysical conclusion are many, and two in particular appeal to me. One is the argument from lan-guage, associated with Wittgenstein; the other is the argument from recognition, associated with Hegel. Both arguments deserve a book-length exposition,

[3] Strawson, "Freedom and Resentment."

and here I must content myself with the briefest summary, in order to suggest that *if* these arguments are valid, then a morality of the I-You relation has just the metaphysical foundation that it needs.

The argument from language tells us that first-person declarations exhibit a special kind of privilege. If I am in pain, then I don't have to find out that I am in pain, and I know that I am in pain on no basis. Not to use the words "I am in pain" in this way is to misunderstand their meaning. In particular it is to misunderstand the word *I*. This word gets its sense from the rule that truthfulness and truth coincide; a speaker who does not obey this rule would be using the term *I* to mean *he* or *she*: the speaker would show that he or she had not grasped the grammar of the first-person case. First-person awareness arises with the mastery of a public language and therefore with the recognition that others are using the word *I* as I do, in order to express what they think and feel directly.

Hegel's argument is similar, though presented in a very different idiom. In the state of nature, motivated only by my desires and needs, I am conscious, but without the sense of self. Through the encounter with the other, which begins in a life-and-death struggle for survival, I am forced to recognize that I too am other to the one who is other to me. Hegel spells out, in poetic steps, the gradual emergence from this encounter of the moment of mutual recognition, in which one comes to know oneself as a free self-consciousness, by recognizing the free self-consciousness that stands

over and against one. Self and other come into consciousness in a single act of recognition, which be-
stows on me the ability to know myself in the first person at the same time as demanding that I recognize
the first-person being of you.[4]

Both arguments acknowledge that first-person
knowledge is peculiarly privileged—a matter not of
observation but of the spontaneous ability to declare,
without evidence, our beliefs, feelings, sensations, and
desires. It is on this spontaneous ability that the I-You
relation is built, and terms such as *I* and *You* get their
sense from the resulting dialogue. But then, do they describe objects in the world of observation? Certainly,
they express the point of view of the subject; but, as we
have seen, subjects are not objects, and points of view
are not *in* the world but *on* the world. Maybe, in any
science of the human species, pronouns would drop
out of consideration altogether. But if that is so, how
can a science of the human being ever reach out to ac-
commodate the moral life, as *we* understand it?

When I talk about myself in the first person, I
utter propositions that I assert on no basis and about
which, over a vast number of cases, I cannot be wrong.
But I can be wholly mistaken about this human being
who is doing the speaking. So how can I be sure that

---

[4]I have expounded both arguments at greater length in *Modern Philosophy* (London: Sinclair-Stevenson, 1994; reissued, London: Blooms-
bury, 2010), chapters 5, 20, and 28. Hegel's argument is expanded,
adapted, and varied in Charles Taylor, *Sources of the Self* (Cambridge,
Mass.: Harvard University Press, 1989).

I am talking about *that very human being*? How do I know, for example, that I am Roger Scruton and not David Cameron suffering from delusions of grandeur? In referring to myself perhaps I am referring to something other than the human being to whom you refer when you point at me: maybe I am doing exactly what I say and referring to a *self*, an entity of which I am immediately and incorrigibly aware.

To cut the story short: by speaking in the first person we can make statements about ourselves, answer questions, and engage in reasoning and advice in ways that bypass all the normal methods of discovery. As a result, we can participate in dialogues founded on the assurance that, when you and I both speak sincerely, what we say is trustworthy: we are "speaking our minds." This is the heart of the I-You encounter. But it does not imply that there is some cryptic entity to which I refer as "I" and which is hidden from your perspective: I am this thing that you too observe and which can be understood in two ways—as an organism and as a person. In addressing me as "you," you address me as a person and are asking me to respond as an "I."

SELF AND OTHER

Kant held that the moral life arises from the subject's self-identification as "I." This idea made a deep impression on his immediate successors, notably on Fichte and Hegel. But they held that my self-identification as "I" is in some deep way dependent on my encounter with and identification of others. From the attempts of the post-Kantian idealists to convey this idea there arose a long tradition that has seen the relation between self and other as the fundamental challenge to philosophy, replacing in this regard the old and discarded problem of the relation between soul and body. And the relation between self and other was further associated, by Hegel, among others, with that between subject and object: between the observer and the observed.

If I were a pure subject, Hegel argues, existing in a metaphysical void, as Descartes imagined, I should never advance to the point of knowledge, not even knowledge of myself, nor should I be able to aim at a determinate goal.[5] My awareness would remain abstract and empty, an awareness of nothing. But I do not merely stand at the edge of my world. I enter that world and encounter others within it. I am I to myself because, and to the extent that, I am you to another. Self-consciousness depends upon the recognition accorded to the self by the other. I must therefore be capable of the free dialogue in which I take charge of my presence before the presence of you. That is what it means to understand the first-person case. And it is because I understand the first-person case that I have

[5] See G.W.F. Hegel, *The Phenomenology of Spirit*, introduction, part A, chapter 4.

immediate awareness of my condition. The position that, for Kant, defines the premise of philosophy, and which is presupposed in every argument, itself rests on a presupposition—the presupposition of the other, the one against whom I try myself in contest and in dialogue. "I" requires "you," and the two meet in the world of objects.

Kant argues persuasively in "The Paralogisms of Pure Reason" that we cannot know the subject under the categories of the understanding—that is, we cannot look inward so as to identify the I as a substance, a bearer of properties, and a participant in causal relations.[6] To identify the subject in that way is to identify it as an *object*. It was Descartes's mistake to look on the subject as a special kind of object and thereby to attribute to it a substantial and immortal nature of its own. The subject is a point of view *upon* the world of objects and not an item *within* it. Kant refers in this connection to the "transcendental subject"—the center of consciousness that lies beyond all empirical boundaries. But this expression, later adopted by Husserl and given a prominent place in Husserlian phenomenology, might seem to imply that we have positive access to the transcendental. Better to refer to the subject as a horizon, a one-sided boundary to the world as it seems.

Nevertheless, even if the subject is not a something, it is not a nothing either. To exist as a subject is

<hr>

[6] Immanuel Kant, *Critique of Pure Reason*, part 2, chapter 1.

to exist in another way than ordinary objects. It is to exist on the edge of the world, addressing reality from a point on the horizon, which no one else can occupy. We each address the world from a standpoint that accords a special and privileged place to our thoughts and feelings. What most matters to me is *present* to me, in thought, memory, perception, sensation, and desire, or can be summoned into the present without any effort of investigation. Moreover, I respond to others as similarly present to themselves, able to answer directly to my inquiries, able to tell me without further inquiry what they think, feel, or intend. Hence we can address each other in the second person, I to you. On those facts all that is most important in the human condition has been built: responsibility, morality, law, institutions, religion, love, and art.

THE INTENTIONALITY OF PLEASURE

Our states of mind have intentionality and therefore depend upon the ways in which we conceptualize the world. Furthermore, we cannot assume that our emotions will remain unaffected when we learn to conceptualize their objects in some new and allegedly "scientific" way. Just as indignation at a villain is undermined by the description of him or her as an automaton obedient to impulses in the central nervous system, so does erotic love retreat when its object is described in the pseudo-scientific jargon of sexology. Maintaining

rewarding human relations—relations that we understand and build upon—means conceptualizing each
other in the ways implied by the honest use of "I" and
"You." It means distinguishing free from unfree actions, reasonable from unreasonable behavior, smiles
from frowns, promises from predictions, contrition
from regret, and so on—through all the complex ways
in which we describe the conduct and responses of
persons as distinct from the conduct and responses of
organisms and of the inanimate world.

It is for this reason that the adaptation story told
by the evolutionary psychologists so often falls short
of explaining them. For such a story will bypass the
"how it seems" of our states of mind, replacing our
own intentional descriptions with neutral scientific
accounts of the kind that could be applied to a dog
or a horse. Nothing illustrates this point more vividly
than the experience of pleasure. An evolutionary theory of pleasure would show why certain things cause
pleasure by explaining the reproductive advantage
conferred on the genes of those who enjoy them. It
would point to the mechanism in the brain that op-
erates whenever enjoyment is felt and which has the
function of turning the organism in the direction of
repeating the experience. It would offer an explanation of addiction, which occurs when a once difficult
reward becomes suddenly easy, so that the path to
reward is, as it were, short-circuited. And it would
explain the difference between constructive and de-
structive pleasures, since adaptive traits can become

maladaptive as conditions change, so that the sweet tooth that ensured our ancestors' survival now condemns us to obesity.

However, we also take pleasure in things that have no obvious evolutionary significance and which it is difficult to connect in any direct way to some original adaptation. We take pleasure in golf, in jokes, in humiliating our enemies; in music, art, and poetry; in stamp collecting, bird-watching, and bungee jumping. Moreover, pleasure is not one thing but many. The pleasure of a warm breeze on the face is a pleasure that we feel *in the face*. There is a place in the body where this pleasure (or maybe we should say "pleasurable sensation") is located. But the pleasures of the table are not like that. The pleasure that we take from the taste of food, for example, is not a "pleasurable sensation in the mouth." There is no exact place where this pleasure is located. Likewise the pleasure in a delightful scent or a fine wine. When it comes to pleasures in visual and auditory impressions, any talk of a place where they are felt, or even of *feeling* at all, seems out of the question. My pleasure in the view from my window is not something that I feel in the eye. It is more like an affirmation of what I see—a joyous recognition that these things before me are good.

Then there are the fully intentional pleasures, which, although in some way tied up with sensory or perceptual experience, are modes of exploration of the world. Aesthetic pleasures are like this. Aesthetic pleasures are contemplative—they involve studying an object *outside* of the self, to which one is *giving* something (namely, attention and all that flows from it), and not *taking*, as in the pleasure that comes from drugs and drinks. Hence such pleasures are not addictive—there is no pathway to reward that can be short-circuited here, and a serotonin injection is not a cheap way of obtaining the experience of *Parsifal* or *The Merchant of Venice*.

Some pleasures are bound up with our evaluations in ways that place them quite beyond the reach of animal minds: the pleasure that a person takes in his or her career, marriage, children, and so on. We are not interested in a successful career or loving marriage in order to feel the pleasure that such things bring; we feel the pleasure (though again, *feel* is not exactly the right word) because we value those things for what they are. The point, already made in other terms by Bishop Butler, is brought home to us by a well-known thought experiment of Robert Nozick.[7] Imagine a device that, when placed on your head, produces all the beliefs and thoughts associated with a successful career, a loving marriage, beautiful children, and whatever else you have ever wanted. Of course this device would produce, in addition to those beliefs, a burst of pleasure. While the device is on top of your head you are on top of the world. But somehow this is not

[7] I have adapted the argument of Robert Nozick, *Anarchy, State, and Utopia* (New York: Basic Books, 1974), pp. 44–45. See the many online discussions of "the experience machine." For Joseph Butler, see his *Fifteen Sermons Preached at the Rolls Chapel* (London, 1729), Sermons 1 and 9.

real pleasure. And the illusory nature of the pleasure means that you would not believe that there is any reason to aim at it. What you want is the *reality* of a successful career, loving marriage, and so on, and the illusion is not a second best but something that it is not rational to want at all.

Among the many other puzzling cases, perhaps the most intriguing is that of sexual pleasure. This is like sensory pleasures in involving body parts, the excitement and tactile stimulation of which are bound up with the pleasure. But it is unlike the normal cases of sensory pleasure in being not only sensitive to thought but also in some way directed *at* or *upon* another person—it seems to have an object or at least is bound up with states of mind that have an object. Hence there can be mistaken sexual pleasures, in which pleasure comes as the result of an error or maybe even a deception. The sleeping woman who is awoken by someone whom she takes to be her husband and with whom she then experiences the pleasure of sex is a case in point. Her pleasure turns quickly to revulsion when she turns on the light. Her pleasure acquires, in retrospect, the character of a hideous mistake. Nor can it be cited in evidence against a charge of rape. This is a pleasure that ought not to have existed, that the woman might want to spit out but cannot, and the revulsion against it may haunt her forever after. Hence Lucretia's suicide. A less drastic case is the pleasure someone might feel at a lover's touch turning instantly to revulsion when he or she learns that the touch is that of an intruder.

SEX, ART, AND THE SUBJECT

That is only a sketch of the many distinctions that we can make, and ought to make, when considering human pleasures. But it already complicates the approach adopted by evolutionary psychology, which sees all pleasure in the same way, as the residue of an adaptive process, whereby an organism became hardwired to behave in ways that further the reproduction of its genes. For my brief survey suggests that pleasures arise in completely different ways and that adaptations that serve one function from the genetic point of view might be put to other uses by our *social* evolution or entirely prized free from their biological function by the demands of individual life.

The example of sexual pleasure is additionally interesting because it concerns a pleasure that is tied up with our nature as reproducing animals. Hence we would be surprised if we could not give an evolutionary account of it. Yet evolutionary accounts seem to fall short of describing what it is that human beings want from sexual activity. Sexual pleasure is focused upon another person, conceived not as an object but as a subject like me. It is not exactly pleasure *over* or *about* the other (and so is not exactly like other emotional pleasures); but it is a kind of pleasure *in* the other. And it is conditional on seeing the other as another—that is to say, not as an object like this (my body) but as a subject like me.

Hence when we encounter forms of sexual interest that are focused on the other as an object (as a this and not a you), we regard them as perverted or forms of abuse.[8] The paradigm case is necrophilia, in which the object of interest is a human being reduced to the status of an object and sex is engaged in as a kind of triumph: a victory over another life. Rape—which is an easy way to genetic investment on the part of the male—also involves a triumph over the other's subjectivity, a delight in wresting sexual pleasure from an unwilling donor. And rape awakens revulsion for that very reason—not just outrage on the victim's behalf but a visceral recoiling from the perpetrator.

As Jonathan Haidt has made clear in his writings on morality, evolutionary psychology makes considerable room for these hard-to-rationalize and instinctive revulsions, such as the revulsion against incest.[9] But it falls short of accounting for their *intentionality*. These revulsions are not just gut reactions, like the revulsion against excrement. They involve the judgment that pleasure is arising in the wrong way, as a pollution of those who pursue it. Evolution tells us that human beings are unlikely to be necrophiliacs—this kind of pleasure is not a good genetic investment— and that we are likely to be repelled by incest. But it won't tell us why incest, rape, pornography, adultery, pedophilia, and a host of other things are regarded as offenses against interpersonal being.

[8] See the discussion in Thomas Nagel, "Sexual Perversion," in *Mortal Questions* (Cambridge: Cambridge University Press, 1979), pp. 39–52.

[9] Jonathan Haidt, *The Righteous Mind: Why Good People Are Divided by Politics and Religion* (London: Allen Lane, 2012).

The same kind of falling short can be observed in evolutionary accounts of aesthetic pleasure—a pleasure that has often been compared with sexual pleasure (as it was, for example, by Plato), since it arises from our delight in the look, feel, sound, and texture of our world. Geoffrey Miller, in his book *The Mating Mind*, makes much of a thought first put about by Darwin, to the effect that the contemplation of appearances might have a role to play in sexual selection. The gorgeous tail of the peacock is a sign of reproductive fitness, precisely on account of its redundancy—only a creature with a good stock of genes could waste so much energy on useless displays. And in his book *The Art Instinct*, Denis Dutton offers to explain our taste in landscapes as being implanted in us by the habitat requirements of Pleistocene man.[10] Our ancestors spent their time looking for places at the edge of the forest, where there was water to drink, open meadows to offer sight of game, and trees in which to escape from predators. So, Dutton says, we should hardly be surprised that landscape paintings with trees, water, and some open vistas are the default preference of people today when it comes to furnishing a room. But again the explanation falls way short of the thing to be explained. The kind of motel kitsch that Dutton is describing is precisely the stuff we learn to discard as we exercise our aesthetic faculties. The person whose

[10] Denis Dutton, *The Art Instinct: Beauty, Pleasure and Human Evolution* (Oxford: Oxford University Press, 2010).

walls are covered with sylvan scenes is one who has yet to learn that aesthetic pleasure involves judgment, discrimination, an ability to distinguish true from fake emotions, a responsible and adult attitude toward the world of nature, and a thousand other things that distance the true goals of art from the survival needs of our hunter-gatherer ancestors.

I don't accept the view that I attributed to Wallace, that there is an impassable gap in the evolutionary process. Language, self-consciousness, moral judgment, aesthetic taste, and so on emerged in some way, and Darwin's suggestion—that things emerge by random variation and survive by selection—has yet to be refuted. But I remain wedded to the old call of philosophy, which tells us to distinguish things and not to elide them and in particular to dwell on those features of our own life that are not to be found among the other animals and which seem to define the human condition as distinct and distinctively meaningful. Even if there is no impassable gap, there is a gap, and it is a significant one.

OVERREACHING INTENTIONALITY

This point is brought home more urgently by what I call the "overreaching intentionality of interpersonal attitudes." In all our responses to each other we look *into* the other, in search of that unattainable horizon from which he or she addresses us. We are objects, caught in the currents of causality, who relate to each other in space and time. But each human object also addresses us in looks, gestures, and words, from the transcendental horizon of the "I."[11] Our responses to others aim toward that horizon, passing on beyond the body to the being that it incarnates. It is this feature of our interpersonal responses that gives such compelling force to the idea of the soul, of the true but hidden self that is veiled by the flesh. And because of this our interpersonal responses develop in a certain way: we see each other as wrapped within them, so to speak, and we hold each other to account for them as though they originated ex nihilo from the unified center of the self.

In addressing you in the second person I at the same time pick you out as a thing that addresses *me* in the second person and who does so only because you identify yourself in the first person. This thought connects with an argument of Elizabeth Anscombe's about intention—in the sense of doing something intentionally or with a particular intention. Anscombe argued that an action is intentional if it admits of the application of a certain sense of the question "Why?" An intentional action is one concerning which the agent can be called upon to give reasons.[12] Intentional actions fall within the sphere of subjective awareness.

[11] See the imaginative argument in J. J. Valberg, *Dream, Death, and the Self* (Princeton: Princeton University Press, 2007).

[12] G.E.M. Anscombe, *Intention* (Oxford: Blackwell, 1957).

I am immediately aware of what I am doing and why, so that you have direct access, through the question "Why?" to my stance toward the world. Of course, there are cases of error, slips of the tongue, and self-deception. But they are deviations from the central case, in which the question "Why?" can be answered immediately, and with a special authority, so that sincerity is a guarantee of truth.

This first-person privilege is so familiar a feature of our mental lives that we do not pause to question it. And attempts to explain it have a tendency to go around in circles or else to take refuge in the idea that I earlier associated with Wittgenstein, that first-person privilege belongs to the "grammar" of self-reference, without telling us exactly what "grammar" in such a context might mean.[13] What is important from the point of view of my argument is that first-person privilege is the foundation of personal relations. In addressing you I am summoning your first-person awareness into the sphere of mine, so to speak. This enables me to discard scientific investigation, psychological theorizing, and the search for hidden motives and to engage with you directly. I can offer you reasons to change your mind or ask for the reasons that will persuade me to change my own. We stand before each other as in a special way in charge of ourselves, our sincere

[13] See Brie Gertler's entry "Self-Knowledge" in the Stanford Encyclopedia of Philosophy for an up-to-date (2015) survey: http://plato.stanford.edu/entries/self-knowledge/.

first-person statements being uniquely authoritative in the revelation of what we think, feel, and do.

Hence the word *you* does not, as a rule, *describe* the other person; it summons him or her into your presence, and this summons is paid for by a reciprocal response. You make yourself available to others in the words that call them to account to you. This would not be possible without the first-person awareness that comes to us with the use of *I*; but that use would in turn not be possible without the dialogue through which we fit together in communities of mutual interest.

An intention is not the same thing as a desire: you can intend to do what you don't want to do and want to do what you don't intend to do. Intending something means being certain that you will do it and also knowing why. Intending is not predicting. I predict that I shall drink too much at the party tonight; but maybe I shall find the strength to go home sober. When making such a prediction I am seeing myself from outside, as it were, assessing the evidence, extrapolating from past observations, and drawing conclusions as I would draw them from observing another. My prediction might turn out to be right or wrong: but it is no more privileged from the point of view of self-knowledge than my predictions about the behavior of someone else. In predicting my behavior "I" becomes "he."

When I *decide* to go home sober I "make up my mind," and this means being certain, on no evidence, that that is what I shall do. In such a case I answer the question "Why?" not by presenting evidence based on past behavior but by offering *reasons for action*. I am *taking responsibility* for my future, and that means bringing it within the purview of first-person knowledge, becoming certain that *that* is what I shall do. If I don't after all go home sober, this is not because I was mistaken in my former assertion about my future action but because I changed my mind.[14]

In the I-You encounter we act for reasons of which we are aware and which the other can ask us to declare. Trust depends on a truthful answer, and here truthfulness is the guarantee of truth. In other words, we can, through our dialogue, directly affect what each of us does. This applies to beliefs, thoughts, and feelings too. And from this ability to account to each other there grows the special kind of relationship of which persons alone are capable. We begin each to take responsibility for what we are, what we do, and what we feel. And by degrees our mutual responsibility is wound into the relation between us, to the point where we undertake the manifold obligations and commitments that distinguish human communities

[14] There is a third possibility, namely, weakness of will, topic of a debate that I am here avoiding. See Donald Davidson, "How Is Weakness of the Will Possible?" in *Essays on Actions and Events*, 2nd ed. (Oxford: Oxford University Press, 2001), pp. 21–42. When I express an intention to do x but do not do it, this cannot be because I made a *mistake* about my own intentions. It is for this reason that weakness of will is a philosophical problem: Exactly *what* goes wrong when it happens?

from all other social networks that we observe. We generate between us what Searle has called "deontic powers," filling our world with obligations that would not exist but for our capacity to invent, accept, and impose them.[15]

It is not that those features of our condition flow from our transcendental freedom, as Kant would put it. They are *what freedom consists in*. Giving each other reasons, holding each other to account, praising, blaming and negotiating, and working for the other's acceptance and being in turn influenced to accept—these are all moments in an ongoing dialogue in which each of us aims attention not to the body of the other but to the first-person perspective that shines in it.

RECENTERING AND DECENTERING THE PASSIONS

Because we call each other to account in this way, our entire emotional life is recentered. It ceases to be attributed to the organism, the "it" that incarnates us, so to speak, but, rather, to the "I" that speaks and looks. By our use of the word *I* we set the body aside, replace the organism with the self, and present to others a target of their interest that is reserved and which must be brought forth in order to treat with those who address

[15] J. R. Searle, *The Construction of Social Reality* (Oxford: Oxford University Press, 1995).

it. That is what I meant when I referred earlier to the overreaching intentionality of interpersonal relations. Others enter into dialogue with this thing called "I" and see it as standing in its sovereign arena, both part of the physical world and situated on its very edge. Of course, it is not a thing in any substantial sense, and readers of Wittgenstein and Hacker will be familiar with the misleading shadows that are cast here by our grammar.[16] Nevertheless, it is true to say that, in a person, states of mind are recentered, self-attributed to the I, so as to become part of the interpersonal dialogue.

The most eloquent illustration of this recentering process is again given by sexual desire. In describing sexual desire we are describing *John*'s desire for *Mary* or *Jane*'s desire for *Bill*. And the people themselves will not merely describe their desires but also experience them in that way: as *my* desire for *you*. "I want you" is not a figure of speech but the true expression of what I feel. And here the pronouns identify that very center of free and responsible choice that constitutes the interpersonal reality of each of us. I want you as the free being that you are, and your freedom is wrapped up in the thing I want, the thing that you identify in the first person, when you engage with me I to I. And that is because I want you to want me in just the same way and likewise to want me to want

[16] P.M.S. Hacker, *Human Nature: The Categorial Framework* (London: Wiley and Sons, 2007).

you, in an escalating mutuality of desire. In popular culture love songs are therefore often elaborations of the second-person pronoun: "All the Things You Are," "I've Got You under My Skin," and so on. And in lyric poetry the second person becomes an invocation, using the familiar form, as in this famous poem of Rückert's:

> Du bist die Ruh,
> Der Friede mild,
> Die Sehnsucht du
> Und was sie stillt.

It is worth recalling the ineffable stillness imparted to those reflections by Schubert, the clever way of condensing an abstract thing yearned for (calm, peace), and even the yearning itself, into the concrete pronoun, which encloses the abstractions and walls them round. *You* here is the transcendental *I* of the other, not describable but the target of my yearning.

Just as our animal feelings can be, and ought to be, recentered in the I, so can those same feelings be decentered, to become spectacles in the world of the "it." That is to say, they can be experienced not as *mine* and as expressions of what I am, what I feel, and what I choose in relating to you but as forces that impinge on me from outside, that prowl like vagabond winds in the world of objects, sweeping I and you away together on the crest of their indifference. Several writers have drawn attention to the objectification of the other, and of women in particular, in the use of pornographic images.[17] There is truth in the complaints, which have their roots in the Kantian intuitions that have animated our secular worldview since the Enlightenment. But I think that the complaints do not get to the heart of the matter. The real evil of porn lies not in its portrayal of other people as sexual objects but in the radical decentering that it effects in the sexual feelings of the observer. It prizes sexual excitement free from the I-You relation and directs it to a nameless scene of mutual arousal, in which arousal too is depersonalized, as though it were a physical condition and not an expression of the self. This decentering of arousal and desire makes them into things that *happen* to me, occurring under the harsh light of a voyeuristic torch instead of being part of what I am to you and you to me, in the moment of intimacy.

This decentering of our vital passions is not confined to the sexual sphere, of course. Nor is the phenomenon entirely new. It is related to what Marx called fetishism and was discerned as such in the art of Hollywood by the somewhat censorious critics of the Frankfurt school.[18] To some extent it has to happen, and it is not always a catastrophe. But we should

[17] Rae Langton, *Sexual Solipsism: Philosophical Essays on Pornography and Objectification* (Oxford: Oxford University Press, 2009).

[18] See, for example, the discussions of cultural fetishism in Theodor Adorno's writings, notably "On the Fetish-Character in Music and the Regression of Listening" (1938), reprinted widely, e.g., in A. Arato and E. Gebhardt, eds., *The Essential Frankfurt School Reader* (New York: Urizen Books, 1978), pp. 270–299.

recognize that if the feelings that serve most to attach us to each other—namely, sexual feelings—are decentered, and if children learn these feelings from their decentered versions, we are bound to experience a vast change in the nature of human communities and in the sentiments on which social reproduction depends.

PERSONAL IDENTITY

So far I have concentrated on the aspect of persons that was brought to the fore by Kant and the post-Kantian idealists—the presence in all of us of the first-person perspective, with its privileged judgments and overreaching intentionality. But there are other aspects too, as a glance at the history of the idea reveals. The term *persona* comes to us from the Roman and Etruscan theater, where it denoted the mask worn by the actor and therefore the character whom the actor portrayed. The term was borrowed by Roman law to describe any entity that has judiciable rights and duties, including corporate entities and other more abstract constructions. It was borrowed again by early Christian theologians in order to explain the doctrine of the Trinity, by distinguishing the three persons of God. Discussions of the Trinity led to the view that personhood belongs to the essence of whatever possesses it, and the sixth-century philosopher Boethius took this as his cue in defining the essential nature of the human being. For Boethius the human person is "an individual substance of a rational nature."[19] That definition was adopted by Aquinas and remained in place until the Enlightenment, when two great philosophers—Locke and Kant—saw fit to reexamine the whole idea and untangle its many strands.

According to Boethius's definition, your being *this person* is what (or who) you essentially are. Hence you could not cease to be this person without ceasing to be. The connection of the person, so defined, with the subject, as described above, is not entirely clear. Nor is it clear how the person is related to the human being. You are essentially this human being and could not cease to be this human being without ceasing to be. But if that is so, must the human being and the person always coexist? Locke raised this question, though not in the terms that I have used, and came to the conclusion that the same person may not be the same human being and vice versa. Others have constructed thought experiments to similar effect—notably Sydney Shoemaker—and the resulting "problem of personal identity" has become a perennial topic of philosophical controversy, with no agreed solution among those who have discussed it.[20]

Similar problems arise in aesthetics. Giorgione's *Tempest* is a particular painting, identified by its pictorial aspect. It is also a physical object situated in the

[19] Boethius, *Liber de Persona et Duabus Naturis*, chapter 3; Aquinas, *Summa Theologiae*, 1, q. 19.

[20] Sydney Shoemaker, *Self-Knowledge and Self-Identity* (New York: Cornell University Press, 1963).

Accademia in Venice. It could not lose its aspect without ceasing to be the work of art that it is. Nor could it cease to be this particular physical object without ceasing to be. But suppose the aspect were transferred by some process onto another canvas and the original painting were destroyed. Does Giorgione's *Tempest* survive or not? Yes, if you count paintings in one way—in terms of their presented aspect; no, if you count them in another way—as physical objects.[21]

Are such paradoxes soluble? In the case of persons we certainly hope so, because the concept of identity over time is vital to our interpersonal relations. In holding each other to account we suppose that we can each affirm identity with a past person, take responsibility for that person's deeds and promises, and also make intentions for the future. Identity across time seems to be fundamental to the concept of the person as we understand it, and indeed all self-attribution presupposes it.[22] Yet the person is anchored in the human being, in something like the way that the *Tempest* is fixed in the specific canvas. And at the same time we can imagine ways in which memory, intention, and accountability flit from body to body or survive the loss of the body entirely, just as we can

[21] See the discussion of the identity conditions for works of art in Richard Wollheim, *Art and Its Objects*, 2nd ed. (Cambridge: Cambridge University Press, 1980).

[22] This has been denied by Derek Parfit, in *Reasons and Persons* (Oxford: Oxford University Press, 1986). Parfit's approach is rebutted by David Wiggins, in *Sameness and Substance Renewed*.

envisage the survival of the body as a self-maintaining organism even when intention, memory, and all other personal faculties have been erased.

Should we be worried by this? My answer is no. The possibility of divergence between our two ways of counting people—as human organisms and as persons—does not subvert the practices that have been built on those rival schemes. We conceptualize the world in two contrasting ways, according to whether our intention is to explain it or to understand it as we understand each other. We cannot live without our interpersonal responses, since they are what we are and all our plans and projects depend on them. But the concepts that they employ have no firm place in the science of our behavior and vanish from the biological theory of the human being, just as the concepts required by the understanding of a painting vanish from the science of pictorial canvases. It remains, therefore, to examine just what our life as persons demands of us.

CHAPTER 3

⌒THE MORAL LIFE⌒

Persons are moral beings, conscious of right and wrong, who judge their fellows and who are judged in their turn. They are also individuals, and any account of the moral life must begin from the apparent tension that exists between our nature as free individuals and our membership of the communities on which our fulfillment depends.

It is sometimes said that the concept of the free individual is a recent invention, a by-product of cultural transformations that might not have occurred and which indeed have not occurred in every part of the world. Jacob Burckhardt argued the point in *The Civilization of the Renaissance in Italy*, the book that founded the discipline of art history as it has been taught in our universities and which fed into the theory of the *Zeitgeist*, inherited from Hegel's philosophy of history.[1] There is truth in Burckhardt's theory,

---

[1] Jacob Burckhardt, *The Civilization of the Renaissance in Italy* (1860; Mineola, N.Y.: Dover Editions, 2010). More radically Sir Larry Siedentop has traced the emergence of the individual to the gospels and the letters of

which describes a culture in which individuals were, perhaps for the first time in Christian civilization, defining their purposes in terms of individual achievement rather than social norms. However, there is also an element of exaggeration. If what I have written in the first two chapters is at all plausible, the habit of self-definition as an individual is part of the human condition itself.

No doubt, in certain circumstances, people come to put a greater emphasis on what distinguishes them from their neighbors than on what they share; no doubt the idea of human life as a single narrative, to be understood as whole in itself, comes to the fore in some epochs and not in others; no doubt the art of some cultures celebrates individuals and their way of "standing out" from the community, while the art of other cultures looks on this posture with indifference or hostility. But in all cases we must distinguish "individualism"—the emphasis on individuals as the creators of their life and its value—from deep individuality—a metaphysical condition that, as persons, we share, whether or not we are also individualists.

DEEP INDIVIDUALITY

We distinguish stuffs from things. Water is a stuff; so too is gold. A ring made of gold is a thing; but it is, as it

---

Saint Paul: *Inventing the Individual: The Origins of Liberalism* (London: Allen Lane, 2014).

were, only accidentally so—it could be melted down to become a link in a chain, or a statuette, or just a lump of gold. Its essence lies in the stuff from which it is composed, and its being this thing rather than that is simply an accident of its history. Other items in our world are things *essentially*: the paradigm being the animals. My horse Desmond is a particular horse; although he is composed of various stuffs—water, flesh, blood—he is essentially this thing, and on ceasing to be this thing he ceases to be. Desmond will one day vanish from the scheme of things. He is identical with himself through time, the enduring substrate of his many changes. And for this reason he would have been described, by Boethius or Aquinas, as an individual substance. Desmond is more of an individual than a stone, since if you divide a stone in two, you still have the same components of the universe— only the arrangement has changed: two bits of stone, rather than one bit. But if you divide Desmond in two, you don't just replace one bit of horse with two bits. You lose the horse. The world after the division is ontologically the poorer, since Desmond the horse has gone.

At the same time, however, Desmond's individuality is, compared with mine, a shallow thing. I am not merely an individual animal, in the way that Desmond is. I identify myself as an individual across time. I take responsibility for my past and make promises for the future: I lay claim to the world as a sphere of my own agency. And my doing this is an expression of the deep individuality that is part of the human condition—which is the condition of a creature that can say "I." This deep individuality is expressed as much in the laws of Hammurabi as in the sonnets of Petrarch, can be read as clearly on an Attic tomb inscription as on a Victorian gravestone, and is a constant of the human condition—the premise of all our hopes and fears and the thing that defines our happiness.

This does not mean that we are unattached atoms, striving for our satisfactions without regard for others. Clearly, if the argument of the last chapter is right, this deep individuality is itself a *social* condition, something that comes about only because individuals are in binding relationships, acknowledging responsibilities, and adopting the second-person standpoint to others as an integral part of adopting the first-person standpoint to themselves. Clearly, therefore, we have the unavoidable question of how to live with others and how to mold our own emotions and habits so as to enjoy their cooperation.

PRAISE, BLAME, AND FORGIVENESS

We do not, when people stand in the way of our appetites, simply sweep them aside, lay hold of the prize, and ignore all rival claims to it. Should we behave in that way, then we will be greeted by hostility and resentment and threatened with punishment. The habit of blaming people arises as a natural offshoot of our competitiveness, and we respond to blame with an excuse, an apology, or an act of repentance. If none of those are forthcoming, the social conditions change. The person who has given offense is now understood in another way, as at war with his or her neighbors. The moral dialogue gives way to a direct confrontation of wills. In the animal kingdom this direct confrontation is the norm, as when rivals dispute over territory or over mates: the conflict continues until the weaker capitulates and gives a sign of defeat.

However, if our first response to injury is not violence but blame, the other is given the opportunity to make amends. Violence is forestalled or postponed, and a process can then begin—the process that is well described in the Roman Catholic theology of repentance—whereby guilty parties are first marginalized and then, through atonement and contrition, reincluded, their fault duly forgiven. It is obvious that communities that have the ability to resolve their conflicts in this way have a competitive advantage over those whose only response to injury is violence. Hence we have here the beginnings of another "adaptation" story of the moral life—though again a story that leaves out the intentionality of our moral responses and the kind of reasoning on which they depend.

Animal communities also have ways of avoiding and overcoming conflict, which to a certain measure mimic the process I have just described. The habit of presenting threats—the pinned-back ears of the horse, the snarl of the dog—prevents violence by warning its potential target. The habit of capitulation rather than fighting to the end over territory and mates likewise has a life-preserving and therefore gene-preserving function. The very fact, made central by Konrad Lorenz, that aggression is by and large toward conspecifics, whose conduct matters in a way that the conduct of other species does not, mimics the forms of human discipline.[2] And many near equivalents of punishment, appeasement, and reconciliation have been observed in our relatives among the apes.[3]

But while these forms of behavior are adaptations (whether of the group or the gene is not important for our purposes), they do not exhibit the kind of reasoning that is exhibited by the moral emotions. When you rightly accuse me of injuring you, I may look for excuses, and there is an elaborate dialogue here through which we express our intuitions concerning the avoidable and the unavoidable.[4] These intuitions are not arbitrary but are based upon a kind of calculus that assesses the extent to which the fault issued from the *will* of the culprit—the extent to which it was the natural result of his or her desires, intentions, and plans, whether or not it was also directly intended. And if I have no excuse, my response

[2] Lorenz, *On Aggression*.

[3] Frans de Waal, *Primates and Philosophers: How Morality Evolved*, ed. Stephen Macedo and Josiah Ober (London: Princeton University Press, 2006).

[4] See J. L. Austin, "A Plea for Excuses," in J. O. Urmson and G. J. Warnock, eds., *Philosophical Papers* (Oxford: Oxford University Press, 1979).

to your accusation will be either to break off relations (which is not a response but an avoidance) or to work for your forgiveness.

Forgiveness cannot be offered arbitrarily and to all comers—so offered it becomes a kind of indifference, a refusal to recognize the distinction between right and wrong. Forgiveness is only sincerely offered by a person who is aware of having been wronged, to another who is aware of having committed a wrong. If the person who has injured you makes no effort to obtain forgiveness and merely laughs at your first moves toward offering it, the impulse to forgive is frozen.[5] If, however, the person apologizes, and if the contrition is proportionate to the offense, a process begins that might have forgiveness as its outcome. The idea of proportionality is important. The person who runs over your child and who then says, "Frightfully sorry," before driving off has not earned your forgiveness. People who take on the full burden of contrition in a case like this must not only try to make amends but also show, through their distress, a full consciousness of the extent to which they have wronged the other, so that their restoration as members of the community must depend on the other's goodwill.

We all have strong intuitions in these matters, and people incapable of the reasoning involved would be

[5] See, for a subtle account of the many complexities here, Charles Griswold, *Forgiveness: A Philosophical Exploration* (Cambridge: Cambridge University Press, 2007).

handicapped in their social relations, perhaps even incapable of entering fully into the life of society. It is true that procedures for assigning responsibility have differed in the many legal systems of which we retain a record.[6] Nevertheless the systems share an emphasis on the will of the perpetrator and the excuses that he or she can offer. People are seldom held liable for a result that they did nothing to cause—for example, an injury to another against whom they were pushed against their will. And all legal systems have a developed account of liability and of the factors that enhance and diminish it.

POLLUTION AND TABOO

There is an interesting exception to this rule, however, vividly apparent in Greek tragedy. Here the offense is one that the victim cannot avoid, since the gods themselves impose it. It is nevertheless the object of shame on the part of the one who commits it. The fault of Oedipus shows him to be an intruder in the community. He is polluted and therefore a fit object of sacrifice. He bears the burden from which the citizens of Thebes can be released when he is cast out from the city and the norms of moral order are restored. He is

---

[6] See Pierre Legrand and Roderick Munday, eds., *Comparative Legal Studies: Traditions and Transitions* (Cambridge: Cambridge University Press, 2011).

shamed before the Thebans and accepts his punishment as rightly inflicted, even inflicts it himself, despite the fact that, to our modern understanding, the punishment is not in any clear sense deserved. Studying such cases, Bernard Williams argues that they convey another conception of liability than the one that weighs with us today.[7] And this might seem to cast doubt upon the thought that there is a natural form of reasoning that guides our allocation of responsibility and our reactions of praise and blame.

When considering Greek tragedy we observe two striking facts: first, that the tragic fault is seen as a *pollution*, by which others might be *contaminated* should it not be purged or purified; second, that the situations portrayed arouse the deepest feelings in us, without our really knowing why. Those facts did not escape the notice of Freud, of course, and he gave a contentious explanation of them. In the Greek tragedy we witness the residue of an older form of moral thinking, an archaeological stratum beneath the realm of personal choice. This older form of thinking, which anthropologists, following Mary Douglas, have called the "ethic of pollution and taboo," sees moral faults as arising as much by contagion as by deed. It emphasizes purity and purification in sexual and familial relations; and it punishes people not by holding them liable for their actions and opening a path to contrition and

---

[7]Bernard Williams, *Shame and Necessity* (Berkeley: University of California Press, 1993).

forgiveness but by casting them out from the community and readmitting them only if some act of purification has changed their status. One might say that the tragic theater takes us into the hunter-gatherer cave, where things long hidden in darkness are briefly revealed, as though by a flash of lightning. The play is an exorcism, arousing fearful spirits, making them briefly visible, and then expelling them in a mystic act of purification. This revisiting of ancient terrors is a part of overcoming them, and it has its equivalent in our own tragic art, as well as our religious rituals.

It is of course reasonable to suppose, with Williams, that our interpersonal morality, in which the will of the individual takes center stage, is simply one possible manifestation of the moral sense. We must be cautious when it comes to generalizing from this instance to claims about other places and times. Nevertheless, even if we admit a measure of historical variation in the way people stand judged before their fellows, the habit of imputing faults, offering excuses, and arguing for the rightness or wrongness of a penalty is universally to be observed, and the difference between an ethic of pollution and taboo and an ethic of accountability is more a matter of emphasis than an absolute divide. In the everyday order of a moral community, assignments of responsibility match diagnoses of the will, the will being understood as the aspect of our activity that issues from the self and which therefore responds to reason. Only when fate or the gods intervene is that order disturbed.

THE SOVEREIGN INDIVIDUAL
AND THE COMMON LAW

In a modern individualistic community, disputes are not settled by dictatorship from some point outside them, and cooperation rather than command is the first principle of collective action. This may not have been the historical norm in human communities, but it is the situation to which our own social impulses direct us, and its emergence as a legally recognized standard of legitimacy is one of the many treasured legacies of the Enlightenment. The Enlightenment idea of the sovereign individual, who confers legitimacy on government by his or her own consent to it, is a generalization of our everyday practice as moral beings. Even under a despotic government, people try to settle their disputes by agreement, upholding promises, making bargains, and imposing penalties on those who default. The bargains may be dangerous, and the law may be inflexible in upholding them, as in *The Merchant of Venice*. But as that play illustrates in so many ways, it is natural to human beings, whatever their political circumstances, to establish their relations by consent and to respect the sovereignty of the individual as the means for achieving this.

The picture that I have been developing of the moral community translates easily into an attendant system of law—the common law whereby disputes and grievances are brought before an impartial judge and resolved according to the ancient principles of natural justice, which advocate the avoidance of bias and the right to a fair hearing. The habit of settling our disputes in that way therefore seems to be a natural adjunct to the moral order. Just those principles that underlie common-law justice in the English-speaking tradition emerge from our spontaneous ways of negotiating solutions to our conflicts. All of the following principles, for example, seem to be accepted by those who lay down their weapons and reason toward solutions instead:

1. Considerations that justify or impugn one person will, in identical circumstances, justify or impugn another.
2. Rights are to be respected.
3. Obligations are to be fulfilled.
4. Agreements are to be honored.
5. Disputes are to be settled by negotiation, not by force.
6. Those who do not respect the rights of others forfeit rights of their own.

Those principles have been taken as defining the field of "natural law," for the reason that their validity depends only on the idea of negotiation itself and not on the circumstances of the one who embarks on it.

Something like this was surely at the back of Adam Smith's mind when, in his *The Theory of Moral Sentiments*, he argued for the "impartial spectator" as the true judge of our moral duties.[8] When asking myself

---

[8] Adam Smith, *The Theory of Moral Sentiments* (London, 1759); reprint of the 1790 edition available from CreateSpace independent publishing platform via Amazon.

what *I* should do, I entertain the thought of what *another* would think of my action when observing it with a disinterested eye. If, as I suggest, morality is rooted in the practice of accountability between self-conscious agents, this is exactly what we should expect. The impartial other sets the standard that we all must meet.

MORAL ARITHMETIC

The conception of the moral life that emerges from the argument that I have been sketching would be called "deontological" by a certain kind of philosopher. That is to say, it presents personal obligation rather than some conception of the overall good as the basic notion of moral reasoning. In this it differs from currently fashionable ways of thinking, such as those advocated by Peter Singer and (somewhat more subtly) Derek Parfit in their recent writings.[9] For Parfit morality is concerned with our duties, but our duties all reduce, in the end, to one, which is the duty to do good—in other words, to obey those "optimific" principles that promise the best outcome in the long run.

For such consequentialist thinkers, all moral problems are, in the end, arithmetical. The entanglements

[9] Peter Singer, *Writings on an Ethical Life* (New York: Ecco, 2000); Derek Parfit, *On What Matters*, 2 vols. (Oxford: Oxford University Press, 2011).

that bind us to each other in specific and historical bonds of right and duty have no secure place in their calculations. Of course others do not matter to us equally, and the many claims on us may be more or less demanding, more or less rewarding, more or less strong. But when it comes to considering *what matters in itself*—in other words, what morality demands of us—such facts, for the consequentialist mind-set, sink into the background, to reappear only as a qualification to other and more abstractly grounded features of our condition. For Singer, Parfit, and many others who speak for our times, the good person is the one who strives for the best outcome in all the moral dilemmas that he or she confronts. And by way of begging the question in favor of their position, they discuss these dilemmas in the form of "trolley problems" and "lifeboat problems." Morality is what guides us in directing a runaway railway trolley from one track to another, when on both tracks a certain number of people are working, or in directing a lifeboat to one group of drowning people or another, in a situation when they cannot all be saved. These "dilemmas" have the useful character of eliminating from the situation just about every morally relevant relationship and reducing the problem to one of arithmetic alone.

Consider the love for our children, which, among normal people, fuses all the circuits in the utilitarian calculator. For Parfit this is just another input into a lifeboat problem. He writes that "the optimific principles would *not* . . . require you to save the strangers rather than your child. If everyone accepted and many people followed such a requirement, things would go in one way better, since more people's lives would be saved. But these good effects would be massively outweighed by the ways in which it would be worse if we all had the motive that such acts would need. For it to be true that we would save several strangers rather than one of our own children, our love for our children would have to be much weaker."[10] And that, Parfit goes on to argue, would have many bad effects in the long run.

What is remarkable about this line of reasoning is that, even if it upholds common sense, it does so on grounds that entirely undermine the obligations on which common sense is founded. It ignores the fact that our children have a claim on us that others do not have and that this claim is *already* a reason to rescue them in their hour of need and requires no further argument. It ignores, one might say, the human reality of the situation that Parfit claims to be imagining, in favor of the spectral mathematics that provides the measure for all his comparative judgments.

COMPARATIVE JUDGMENTS

On the other hand, it is true that we make comparative judgments, and it is a powerful argument for consequentialism that it makes sense of this. Deontological accounts of morality, such as Kant's, seem, at

[10] Parfit, *On What Matters*, vol. 1, p. 385.

times, to take little account of our comparative ways of thinking and also to have great difficulty in explaining them. In our most urgent moral dilemmas we ask ourselves which of two courses of action would be *better* or which among a number of actions would be *best*. This fact is easily dealt with on a consequentialist view—too easily, some would say. Consequentialists treat moral reasoning like economic reasoning and sometimes spell out their thoughts in terms of preference orderings and their aggregation.[11] The temptation then is to graft as much mathematics as we can onto our moral discourse and to rewrite morality as "moral arithmetic," to use an expression put to a related use by Buffon. The trolley problems do this for Parfit. As the examples unfold, and the mathematics takes over, the relation to ordinary moral thought becomes more and more strained.[12]

Here is one of the cases that Parfit invokes: "If we choose A Tom will live for 70 years, Dick will live for 50 years, and Harry will never exist. If we choose B Tom will live for 50 years, Dick will never exist, and

[11] As, for example, in John Broome, *Weighing Lives* (Oxford: Oxford University Press, 2004).

[12] Interestingly, the revulsion against "mathematical" moral problems, which we find among anticonsequentialist thinkers such as Elizabeth Anscombe (G.E.M. Anscombe, "Modern Moral Philosophy," *Philosophy* 33, no. 124 [1958]: pp. 1–19) and vehemently expressed by Allen Woods in his response to Parfit (included in vol. 2 of *On What Matters*), is shared by R. M. Hare, who thinks of trolley problems as the recourse of the anticonsequentialists in their last-ditch attempts to resist the inevitable triumph of utilitarianism. See R. M. Hare, *Moral Thinking: Its Levels, Method and Point* (Oxford: Oxford University Press, 1981), p. 139.

Harry will live for 70 years."[13] So should we choose A or B? With relentless determination Parfit conducts the reader through case after case of this kind, arguing that Scanlon's view, that reasons are inherently *personal*, will not account for all the many instances in which we might be called upon to make a moral choice.[14] But the importation of precision does not hide the fact that the examples considered are entirely unlike real moral dilemmas and entirely shaped by the arithmetical obsession of their author. Real dilemmas come about in the way that Scanlon says they do, from what we owe to each other or, to use the terms I have adopted, from the ways in which we hold ourselves and others to account. A spectral version of moral reasoning can survive in the world of the trolley problems; but it exists there detached from its roots in the person-to-person encounter, lending itself to mathematical treatment partly because the deskbound philosopher has thought the normal sources of moral sentiment away.

That is not to deny that moral reasoning makes comparisons. When Anna Karenina asks herself whether it is right to leave Karenin and to set up house with Vronsky, she is asking herself which of two courses of action would be *better*. But although she is making a comparative judgment, it is not one that

---

[13] Parfit, *On What Matters*, vol. 2, p. 223; format modified.

[14] T. M. Scanlon, *What We Owe to Each Other* (Cambridge, Mass.: Harvard University Press, 1998).

can be resolved by a calculation. She is torn between her obligations to her husband and child and her love for Vronsky. Her dilemma is not detachable from its peculiar circumstances—her husband's vindictiveness and coldness of heart, her son's sweet devotion, Vronsky's *Leichtsinn*, and Anna's knowledge of his faults. Dilemmas of this kind exist because we are bound to each other by obligations and attachments, and one way of being a bad person is to think they can be resolved by moral arithmetic. Suppose Anna were to reason that it is better to satisfy two healthy young people and frustrate one old one than to satisfy one old person and frustrate two young ones, by a factor of 2.5 to 1: ergo I am leaving. What would we think, then, of her moral seriousness?

CONSEQUENTIALISM AND THE MORAL SENSE

That is but one reason for thinking that the idea of an "optimific principle" is both obscure in itself and unable to do the work that consequentialists require of it. Take away the trolleys and the lifeboats and we rarely know how to calculate "the best," either in the particular case or when considering the application of principles. The consequences of our actions stretch infinitely outward in both space and time. The best of intentions can lead to the worst of results. And values are many and in tension with each other. What place should we accord to beauty, grace, and dignity—or do these all creep into our deliberations as parts of human happiness? There is no knowing how either Parfit or Singer would answer such a question, for their writings are devoid of moral psychology and have little or nothing to say about what happiness consists in, by what scale it should be measured, or what human beings gain from their aesthetic and spiritual values.

Moreover both philosophers overlook the actual record of consequentialist reasoning. Modern history presents case after case of inspired people led by visions of "the best," believing that all rational beings would adopt those visions if only they would think about them clearly. *The Communist Manifesto* is one such vision. It gives a picture of "the best" and argues that all would work for it, the bourgeoisie included, if only they understood the impeccable arguments for its implementation. Those who stand in the way of revolution are self-interested; but they are also irrational and would change sides if they thought seriously about principles that everyone could will to be laws. Since their interests prevent them from thinking in that way, violent revolution is both necessary and inevitable.

Lenin and Mao, who put this document into practice, were adept at trolley problems. The moral arithmetic always came out in their favor, as they switched the trolley of history from one set of possible victims to another. And when the fat man had to be pushed from the bridge, there was always someone ready to do the job for them, who could be pushed from the bridge in turn. The result was the total destruction of two great societies and irreversible damage to the rest of us. Why suppose that we, applying our minds to the question of what might be best in the long run, would make a better job of it? Moreover, is not this possibility—indeed probability—of error at the root of what is so objectionable in consequentialism, which turns wrongdoing into an intellectual mistake, thereby excusing it? When the Kaiser, looking back on the calamity of World War I, said, "Ich hab' es nicht gewollt," he spoke as a consequentialist, as did all those apologists who regretted the "mistakes" of Lenin and Mao.

Which brings me back to the question of motives. The fundamental intuition behind my argument in this essay is that morality exists in part because it enables us to live on negotiated terms with others. We can do this because we act for reasons and respond to reasons too. When we incur the displeasure of those around us, we attempt to justify our actions, and it is part of our accountability that we should reach for principles that others too can accept and which are perforce impartial, universal, and lawlike. When the fault is ours we blame ourselves, and good people blame themselves more severely than others would. We recognize obligations to those who depend on us and on whom we depend, and we exist at the center of a sphere of accountability, which stretches out from us with dwindling force across the world of other people. Our moral principles are the precipitate of personal relations, in which we are face-to-face with those who have a claim on us and who are more interested in our virtues and vices than in our ability to derive output from input on our pocket moral calculators. Hence what Strawson calls "reactive attitudes"—including guilt, admiration, and blame—form the core of our moral sentiments, bearing the indelible mark of the I-You relations in which they are ultimately rooted.[15]

To give a full account of what this involves we must go beyond the emphasis on advocacy and the resolution of conflict. Morality governs each personal encounter, and its force radiates from the other. In seeking the motive of our moral behavior, therefore, we must understand what is involved in the relation between beings who identify themselves in the first person and who address the first person of the other: the relation based on the overreaching intentionality that I described in the second chapter. Contracts arise as a special case of this "transcendental" encounter. But they are not the only case: people come to depend on each other in many ways, and from the point of view of morality it is often the noncontractual forms of dependence that are the most significant—family relations, warfare, duties of charity, and justice toward strangers.

VIRTUE AND VICE

Light is shed on this matter if we return to a conception of the moral life that is associated with Aristotle, since he defended it in his own terms in the *Nicomachean Ethics*. According to this conception the key to

[15] Strawson, "Freedom and Resentment."

the moral life is virtue, and for Aristotle virtue consists in the ability to pursue what reason recommends, despite the motives that strive against it. The point can be put in the language that I have been using thus: virtue consists in the ability to take full responsibility for one's acts, intentions, and avowals, in the face of all the motives for renouncing or denouncing them. It is the ability to retain and sustain the first-personal center of one's life and emotions, in face of the decentering temptations with which we are surrounded and which reflect the fact that we are human beings, with animal fears and appetites, and not transcendental subjects, motivated by reason alone.

Ancient thinkers distinguished four cardinal virtues—courage, prudence, temperance, and justice—and with adjustments and refinements, their account of the matter has stood the test of time. Courage provides the simplest and clearest example. The soldier fighting beside his companions is afraid, as they are, of injury and death. In the worst moments of battle he may be sorely tempted to run for safety. But his duty forbids this. His duty is to stand and fight, to protect his companions, and to commit himself to the cause of honor. This duty is something that he owes, and as many observers have confirmed, even if the obligation is rationalized as something owed to a country, a cause, or an ideal, it is experienced first and foremost as something owed to his companions, to those who share the risk of fighting, to whom he is *semper fidelis*, as expressed in the motto ("Semper fi") of the American marines. It is not a contractual duty, and there is no "deal" that could summarize its terms. It arises as the lived sense of commitment to others, in whose eyes the soldier is judged.

In these circumstances the soldier must *silence* his fear, so that only the call of duty can be heard. Acceptable reasons for action are centered in the "I." They are reasons that can become *my* reasons, the reasons that would both explain what I do and justify it in the eyes of anyone to whom I consider myself accountable. These reasons stem from "what I truly am to myself" rather than from "the forces that act on me."[16] Fear, for the soldier, is therefore something to be *overcome*, which does not mean that he should blithely court danger or ignore the fact that he *is* afraid and with good reason; it means, rather, that the considerations that justify his fear should not be allowed to prevail over what he *must* do in his own eyes and in the eyes of the world.

HONOR AND AUTONOMY

Kantians would argue that, in such a case, the soldier should be motivated by reason, acting out of "autonomy of the will." It is what the soldier sees to be right that provides both his justification and his motive.

---

[16] Hence, in Christine Korsgaard's reconstruction of the Kantian moral philosophy, the authority of practical reasons derives ultimately from the agent's conception of his or her identity. See Christine Korsgaard, *Self-Constitution: Agency, Identity and Integrity* (Oxford: Oxford University Press, 2009).

Rival motives, which owe their force to emotions that operate outside the will, are discounted: to give way to them is tantamount to "heteronomy of the will," the great sin against the self that points the way to the decentering that I described in the second chapter. The autonomous motive has a lawlike character: that, for Kant, is what the word *ought* means—namely, that the action is being prescribed as necessary. Through our passions we are subject to the "causality of nature"; but there is also, for Kant, a "causality of reason" that acts on us in another way and from another and, as it were, transcendental perspective.

Kant's tight knot of argument is difficult to untie, but it seems to capture many of our intuitions about the peculiar force of morality and about the way in which the sense of duty sets us outside and against the order of nature. We are law-governed creatures, and even when we defy the law, we act on the assumption that we are subject to nonnegotiable demands—reasons that have the power to silence countervailing considerations, however closely they represent our empirical interests.

In fact we do not need to suppose a "causality of reason" in order to make sense of the soldier's predicament. We need only recognize that the soldier, like every person, has a sense of obligation—a sense of promises given and received, of relations to others that depend on his loyalty, of responsibilities undertaken, all of which are stored in his thinking in a place apart. These things are stored in the I, as commitments "to be honored," and have a distinct status in defining the soldier's sense of who he is. To dishonor them is possible; but the price of doing so is guilt, remorse, and adverse judgment of the self by the self, such as blighted the life of Conrad's Lord Jim.[17]

Aristotle argued that courage requires the ability to pursue what honor requires despite the countervailing considerations of fear and rage. He also argued that this ability is a disposition—a *hexis*—not different in kind from the motives that conflict with it. Unlike Kant, Aristotle did not recognize reason as a metaphysically *distinct* motive; but he did think that the disposition to follow what reason commands is a *real* motive, one that depends on cultivating good habits and one that puts the agent in the very position that Kant sees as central to the moral life: the position of honoring obligations, despite the passions that oppose them.

Aristotle also claimed that all the cardinal virtues share the structure of courage. Each such virtue involves a disposition to pursue what reason acknowledges to be honorable or right, in the face of countervailing temptations. This disposition is acquired through imitation and the awareness of being judged. Virtues are dispositions that we praise, and their absence is an object of shame. To put the matter in the

---

[17] Joseph Raz has argued that these "preemptive reasons" are fundamental to the very idea of law, as a distinct form of authority in practical reasoning. See his *The Authority of Law*, 2nd ed. (Oxford: Oxford University Press, 2009).

terms that I have been using, it is through virtue that our actions and emotions remain centered in the self, and vice means the decentering of action and emotion, so that the I and its undertakings no longer have the central or controlling place in determining what one feels and does. Vice is, literally, a loss of self-control, and the vicious person is the one on whom we cannot rely in matters of obligation and commitment.

MRS. JELLYBY AND THE GOOD SAMARITAN

If we accept that broad picture of the moral life, then we can see how far from ordinary morality are the consequentialist prescriptions of Singer and Parfit. The point was made vividly by Dickens, in the character of Mrs. Jellyby in *Bleak House*, whose self-congratulatory posture as a do-gooder, dedicated to improving the situation of the natives of Borrioboola-Gha, coexisted with her neglect of all those who directly depended on her and for whom she was responsible—her children in particular. Nor did the actual consequences of Mrs. Jellyby's actions provide any vindication of them, since the despot of Borrioboola-Gha merely kidnapped her volunteers and sold them into slavery. And how was she to know that he wouldn't do that?

There is no evidence that a university professor who has thought long and hard about improving the world, as Singer has, will be any better at calculating the consequences of a given policy than Mrs. Jellyby.

Consider some of the issues discussed by Singer: abortion, euthanasia, eating animals. How do we compare the long-term happiness of societies in which abortion is allowed with the long-term happiness of those in which it is forbidden? Only the feeblest first moves can be made, as in Parfit's justification, above, for a morality that makes room for the love of children, a justification that would have cut no ice against Plato's similarly consequentialist argument for making children the property of the state. Compared with our immediate obligations, founded in relations of accountability and dependence, consequentialist arguments have an arbitrary appearance and depend for their credibility on a hypothesis about consequences that is rarely more than wishful thinking.

This does not mean that we are free to ignore the consequences of our actions, or that we should not strive for the best outcome of our moral choices, for in this respect too we are judged; nor does it mean that we must allow our duties, however minor, to outweigh the good that can be self-evidently achieved by ignoring or overriding them. It means, rather, that consequential reasoning must take second place in our worldview to the obligations that create the motivational heart of the moral life. If we do not acknowledge this, then we might end with a purely intellectual morality, one that permits us to excuse any action whatsoever as a "mistake" of reasoning and to recommend any course of action regardless of the claims that others have on our concern. Or if we do not take that route, and we become Jellybists instead, we might find ourselves floundering under impossible burdens, in the vain attempt to know what is the best way to use our energies and powers in the cause of "doing good" and then to devote our lives to doing it.[18]

There is an interesting contrast here between two possible readings of Christ's parable of the Good Samaritan, given in answer to the question "Who is my neighbor?" The orthodox reading tells us that Christ was telling us to ignore distinctions of ethnicity and faith and to do good to others in an impartial and universal way. From this reading it is possible to derive a consequentialist morality, which advocates optimal solutions to our moral dilemmas and ignores those historically incurred obligations that cause us to distinguish between people and communities. But there is another and in my view more plausible reading, according to which the Samaritan finds himself confronted with a *specific* obligation to a *specific* person. His assistance is offered in response to an individual need; it is not a contribution to the sum of the good but an obligation to a fellow human being who is appealing immediately for help. Having undertaken this obligation the Samaritan then recognizes that it is not fulfilled merely by first aid. After transporting the victim to an inn and paying for his succor there, the

[18] For some fascinating cases of martyrs to Jellybism, see Larissa Mac-Farquhar, *Strangers Drowning: Voyages to the Brink of Moral Extremity* (London: Allen Lane, 2015).

Samaritan returns to see how he is getting on. He undertakes a concrete commitment and recognizes that he must see the matter through.

On this second reading of the parable, the moral life is represented roughly as I have described it, as rooted in personal obligations. On the first reading it is quite possible to think that the Samaritan, having applied first aid, did wrong to spend so much of his money and time on the victim, instead of sending his money to the people of Borrioboola-Gha.

RIGHTS, DESERTS, AND DUTIES

There is a kind of "calculus of rights and duties" that we rational beings use in order to settle our disputes with each other and to reach agreement over matters of common or conflicting interest. The concept of justice belongs to this calculus, and its use enables people to claim a sphere of personal sovereignty in which their choice is law. This means that, in a deontological morality of the kind I have been advocating, concepts such as right and desert will have an important role. By determining our rights and deserts we define the fixed points, the places of security, from which people can negotiate and agree. Without those fixed points negotiation and free agreement are unlikely to occur, and if they occur, their outcome is unlikely to be stable. If I have no rights, then the agreement between us provides no guarantee of performance; my sphere of action is liable to constant invasion by others, and there is nothing that I can do to define my position in a way that compels you to acknowledge it. Likewise, without a concept of desert, settling the question of when punishment is appropriate or proportionate, a vital shield is removed from the individual, exposing him or her to every kind of coercion.

Rights and deserts, then, enable us to establish a society in which consensual relations are the norm, and they do this by defining for each of us a sphere of personal sovereignty from which others can be excluded. And rights and deserts define duties too. My right is your duty, and if I do not deserve what you do to me, then you have no right to inflict it. When we refer to rights, deserts, and duties; what we owe to each other; and such fundamental ideas as freedom, justice, and the impartial spectator, we are making use (directly or indirectly) of the concept of the person, which provides the shared perspective from which we address virtually all such issues. Human communities are communities of persons, and this is the point of agreement from which our disagreements begin.

For those and related reasons, getting clear about the concept of the person is, for us, an intellectual priority. Those who build a universal political doctrine on the foundation of human rights are in need of a theory that tells them which rights belong to our nature—our nature as persons—and which are the product of convention. That theory will be a theory of the person. Marxists who found their critique of bourgeois society on the idea of exploitation and the dignity of labor rely on the view that there is a fulfilled and free relation between people, which the capitalist system suppresses. That view demands a theory of the person. Theists see the goal of human life as the knowledge and love of a personal God, whose presence is revealed in the natural order. We can make sense of that view only if we have a theory of the person. Left-liberals see political order as a mechanism for reconciling individual freedom with "social justice." That idea too depends on a theory of the person. The allegedly Kantian philosophy of the person assumed by John Rawls in his defense of the redistributive state is used by Robert Nozick to attack it. In every area of political conflict today we find the concept of the person at the center of the dispute yet treated as a mere abstraction, with little or no attention to its social and historical context.

THE PERSON AND THE SELF

If the defining feature of the human person is the freedom to make autonomous choices, then libertarians will argue that governments and civil associations have no right to interfere with those choices, save on the ground proposed by John Stuart Mill, of protecting others from harm.[19] If the defining feature of the

---

[19] See the argument of John Stuart Mill, *On Liberty* (London, 1859).

human person is, rather, life in a community of mutual aid, then communitarians will argue that we must constrain antisocial lifestyles and provide for a society in which caring is an institutional fact. These conflicting accounts of the person arise because thinkers have taken the concept out of context, seeking to define it in abstract terms and without reference to the way in which personhood is a way of *becoming*, not just a way of being. Libertarians emphasize freedom but give us no real account of the origins of freedom or its metaphysical basis. Communitarians emphasize social dependence but fail to explore the difference between the groupings of animals and those of free beings, whose associations are founded in contract and consent and whose social fulfillment comes only in the mutual recognition of their individual autonomy.

It has been my contention that these conflicts can be understood and to a great measure resolved once we understand the root of the concept of the person in the I-You encounter and the priority of first-person knowledge both in creating the relations between us and in showing us exactly who and what we are. Personal relations are a *calling to account*. I am answerable to you for what I say and do, and you likewise to me. To put it in Hegel's way, we are subjects for each other, not objects, and the subject-to-subject encounter is one of mutual recognition, in which each acknowledges the other's autonomy and also holds others responsible for what they are and do. My freedom is not an uncaused eruption into the world of human events; it is a product of my social condition, and it brings with it the full burden of responsibility to the other and the recognition that the other's voice has just as much authority as mine.

If this is so, then we should conclude that the libertarian and the communitarian each give one-half of the truth. Freedom and accountability are coextensive in the human agent. And the dialogue through which we address each other involves a search for reasons that have weight for you as much as for me. There is, at the heart of the human community, the "common pursuit" of reasons that will be valid for all of us. Next time you have a quarrel with someone, you can test this out. You will find that you seek to justify yourself with reasons that the other will accept, whose validity does not depend on the particular desires that distinguish you but, rather, on matters that lie rooted in your shared human nature and shared social circumstances. Freedom and community are linked by their very nature, and the truly free being is always taking account of others in order to coordinate his or her presence with theirs.

To develop fully as persons, I have argued, we need the virtues that transfer our motives from the animal to the personal center of our being—the virtues that put us in charge of our passions. These virtues are not available outside a tightly woven social context. Without socially endorsed forms of education, without families and spheres of mutual love, without the disciplined approach to erotic encounters, our social emotions will surely not be fully centered in the "I." Human beings find their fulfillment in mutual love and self-giving, but they get to this point via a long path of self-development, in which imitation, obedience, and self-control are necessary moments. This is not a hard thing to understand once we see the development of personality in the terms suggested by Aristotle. But it is a hard thing to practice. Nevertheless, when we understand things rightly, we will be motivated to put virtue and good habits back where they belong, at the center of personal life.

CHAPTER 4

⁓SACRED OBLIGATIONS ⁓

Not all American moral philosophers are consequentialists in the mold of Singer. It is more common to
be a "contractarian," for whom morality is a system of
interpersonal coordination among people with po-
tentially competing "conceptions of the good." The
underlying justification for this position may indeed
have a consequentialist element, holding that moral
thinking inculcates habits of respect and benevolence
that guarantee general safety. But in itself morality
consists in the "side constraints," to use Nozick's expression, that make agreement rather than coercion
into the foundation of our social conduct. These side
constraints are embodied in a system of rights and
duties: around each individual is a wall of rights that
protect him or her from unjust coercion, and on every
individual is imposed a set of duties by which those
rights are guaranteed.

Current political philosophy begins from a similar
picture but goes one stage further, exploring the virtues of a benevolent state and usually making social
justice, sometimes liberty, into the overarching aim of

government. For both moral philosophy and political philosophy, as these are taught in the modern academy, the critical instruments of social coordination are the system of rights and duties, the virtues that motivate us to obey it, and the political backing that makes obedience possible and which coordinates our many and diverse projects. The political order supplements morality with a positive law designed to guarantee our freedom and to rectify the systemic injustices that arise through its exercise. The moral law and the positive law are in turn justified by abstract theories, which are understood entirely in terms of individual autonomy and the freedoms and rights implied by it.

That picture, with of course many subtle additions and qualifications, underlies Rawls's *A Theory of Justice* and Nozick's *Anarchy, State, and Utopia*, along with the vision of human beings assumed in the legal philosophy of Ronald Dworkin and Joseph Raz and in the moral philosophy of Tim Scanlon.[1] From David Gauthier's *Morals by Agreement* and Loren Lomasky's *Persons, Rights, and the Moral Community* to Stephen Darwall's *The Second-Person Standpoint* and Martha Nussbaum's *Frontiers of Justice*,[2] we find near-universal agreement among American moral

---

[1] John Rawls, *A Theory of Justice* (Oxford: Oxford University Press, 1971; revised ed., 1999); Nozick, *Anarchy, State, and Utopia*.

[2] David Gauthier, *Morals by Agreement* (Oxford: Oxford University Press, 1986); Loren Lomasky, *Persons, Rights, and the Moral Community* (Oxford: Oxford University Press, 1987); Darwall, *The Second-Person Standpoint*; Martha Nussbaum, *Frontiers of Justice: Disability, Nationality, Species Membership* (Cambridge, Mass.: Harvard University Press, 2006).

philosophers that individual autonomy and respect for rights are the root conceptions of moral order, with the state conceived either as an instrument for safeguarding autonomy or—if given a larger role—as an instrument for rectifying disadvantage in the name of "social justice." The arguments given for these positions are invariably secular, egalitarian, and founded in an abstract idea of rational choice. And they are attractive arguments, since they seem to justify both a public morality and a shared political order in ways that allow for the peaceful coexistence of people with different faiths, different commitments, and deep metaphysical disagreements. The picture of the moral life that I have presented is largely compatible with these arguments. But it also points to two important criticisms that might be made of them.

TWO CRITICISMS

The first criticism is that the contractarian position fails to take our situation as organisms seriously. We are embodied beings, and our relations are mediated by our bodily presence. All of our most important emotions are bound up with this: erotic love, the love of children and parents, the attachment to home, the fear of death and suffering, the sympathy for others in their pain or fear—none of these things would make sense if it were not for our situation as organisms. The love of beauty, too, has its roots in our embodied life and in the here and now of our joys. If we were disembodied rational agents—"noumenal selves" of the kind that would be at home in Kant's Kingdom of Ends—then our moral burdens would be lightly worn and would amount only to the side constraints required to reconcile the freedom of each of us with the equal freedom of our neighbors. But we are embodied beings, who are drawn to each other as such, trapped into erotic and familial emotions that create radical distinctions, unequal claims, fatal attachments, and territorial needs, and much of moral life is concerned with the negotiation of these dark regions of the psyche.

The second criticism is that our obligations are not and cannot be reduced to those that guarantee our mutual freedom. Noumenal selves come into a world unencumbered by ties and attachments for the very reason that they do not come *into* the world at all. They are without a situation, except insofar as they themselves create one, through their free activity among others who are in the same unanchored state. For us humans, who enter a world marked by the joys and sufferings of those who are making room for us, who enjoy protection in our early years and opportunities in our maturity, the field of obligation is wider than the field of choice. We are bound by ties that we never chose, and our world contains values and challenges that intrude from beyond the comfortable arena of our agreements. In the attempt to encompass these values and challenges, human beings have developed concepts that have little or no place in liberal theories of the social contract—concepts of the sacred and the sublime, of evil and redemption, that suggest a completely different orientation to the world than that assumed by modern moral philosophy.

The most important challenge facing my account of the moral life is to answer those two objections. I must show how the embodied and situated nature of the human agent can be acknowledged in our moral thinking, how unchosen obligations are shaped and justified, and how the experiences of evil and the sacred contribute to our overall consciousness of what matters. In chapter 3 I remarked on the situations explored in Greek tragedy, which seem to present a rival concept of guilt and liability to that emerging from modern theories of the person. The ethic of pollution and taboo, or "shame and necessity," which sees evil as a contamination and associates evil at every point with our bodily condition, seems better placed to deal with sexual transgression, with our duties toward the dead and the unborn, and with the experiences of the sacred, the sacrificial, and the desecrated that stir such powerful currents of emotion in us all. But that ethic is without any clear philosophical foundation and goes radically against my attempt to found morality in interpersonal relations.

SEXUAL MORALITY

In his pioneering study *Sexual Ethics*, first published in 1930, Aurel Kolnai argued that sexual morality can be derived neither from a study of costs and benefits, in the consequentialist manner, nor from the Kantian categorical imperative, with its emphasis on the self and the will.[3] The core concept in any sexual ethic worth the name, Kolnai believed, is that of dirt or defilement (*das Schmutzig*). Kolnai did not express the matter in the anthropological terms that I have used. Nevertheless, he remained convinced that this feeling of defilement is an objective indicator of what is at stake in sexual desire and its expression. And it was, for Kolnai, the premise in an argument designed to vindicate the Roman Catholic view of chastity, priesthood, and marriage.

Insofar as sexual morality is discussed by modern moral philosophers, the idea of defilement seems to have no clear place. The task of philosophy is often seen as one of "freeing up" the sexual impulse for guilt-free enjoyment, by debunking the superstitions that have been heaped across the path of our pleasures.[4] The crucial matter, as in all contractarian approaches, is that of consent—informed consent between the partners being regarded as the necessary (and for many thinkers the sufficient) condition for legitimate sexual relations. If consensual sex is ever condemned on this view, it is because the consent of

---

[3] Aurel Kolnai, *Sexual Ethics: The Meaning and Foundations of Sexual Morality*, trans. Francis Dunlop (London: Ashgate, 2005).

[4] Examples include Igor Primoratz, *Ethics and Sex* (London: Routledge, 1999); Richard Posner, *Sex and Reason* (Cambridge, Mass.: Harvard University Press, 1992); Alan Soble, *Sex from Plato to Paglia: An Encyclopedia*, 2 vols. (Westport, Conn.: Greenwood Press, 2006); and so on.

one party has been obtained by manipulation or by the abuse of power, as between teacher and pupil or doctor and patient. The suggestions that certain partners are forbidden (because they are of the wrong sex or in the wrong organic relation or wrongly situated in the social world), that sex within marriage is morally of a different kind than sex outside marriage, or that there are real temptations that should be resisted, even when the temptation is mutual—all such suggestions seem groundless, mere superstitions hanging over from an unenlightened age.

That said, it is surely true that those who deny themselves concepts of defilement and desecration cannot begin to encompass the feelings of a woman who is a victim of rape. Forced against her will to experience her sex as a bodily function rather than a gift of herself, she feels assaulted and polluted in her very being. And how the victim *perceives* the act is internally connected to what the act *is*. The sense of pollution and desecration is not an *illusion* on the victim's part: it is an accurate perception of what has been done to her, and deliberately done. If we are to follow the account of sexual interest and sexual pleasure purveyed by the standard literature, however, this perception must appear entirely irrational, and rape victims who make a fuss must be compared with people who try to sue those who bump into them in the street. (By standard literature I mean the well-known current of thinking that received such a sudden inflation with the Kinsey Report, the philosophy behind which is epitomized in the encyclopedia by Alan Soble entitled *Sex from Plato to Paglia*.)

Likewise with incest. You can feel sympathy toward Siegmund and Sieglinde in *Die Walküre* because they recognize their consanguinity only in a state of mutual arousal—and then nobly endorse it as an act of defiance. They had not shared a home, and their siblinghood dawns on them in the course of their desire for each other. Such exceptional cases apart, incest gives rise to profound qualms in almost all of us. Freud gave an explanation of this, arguing that the revulsion against incest is a defense against a deep desire to do it. Evolutionary psychology gives another and conflicting explanation—namely, that this revulsion is an adaptation. Genes that do not produce it in their human avatars have all died out. But neither Freud nor evolutionary psychology puts us in touch with the moral heart of the matter—which is the experience of revulsion itself, the experience that we conceptualize in the way I have suggested, through notions of pollution and desecration. Those conceptions explain why Jocasta hanged herself and why Oedipus stabbed out his eyes. In comparison neither Freud nor evolutionary psychology makes sense of what is—from their rival points of view—highly eccentric behavior.

Modern philosophy agrees that personhood is a central moral category—maybe the qualification for entry into the realm of moral subjects. And many philosophers acknowledge that personhood is a relational idea: you are a person to the extent that you can participate in the network of interpersonal relationships that I described in the second chapter. To be a person, therefore, you must have the capacities that make those relationships possible. These include self-awareness, accountability, and practical reason. Persons fall under the scope of Kant's moral law: they must respect each other as persons. In other words, they should grant to each other a sphere of sovereignty. Within your sphere of sovereignty what is done, and what happens to you, insofar as it depends on human choices, depends on choices of yours. As I argued in chapter 3, this can be guaranteed only if people are shielded from each other by a wall of rights and protected from aggression by a concept of desert. Without rights and deserts individuals are not sovereigns but subjects. These rights and deserts are inherent in the condition of personhood and not derived from any convention or agreement. In other words they are "natural."

But none of that explains the revulsion against rape. The concept of a natural right is too formal a notion: it tells us that a person has a right not to be raped, since rape casts aside consent, rides over the will, and treats the other person as a means to pleasure. All bad, of course. But the same offense is committed by the one who hugs a person against his or her will or who, unknown to another person and in a state of excitement, watches that person undress. Without the element of pollution we have not identified the real measure of the crime.

This does not mean that the morality of interpersonal respect is irrelevant. On the contrary, it accounts for many of our moral intuitions. But the abstract liberal concept of persons as centers of free choice, whose will is sovereign and whose rights determine our duties toward them, delivers only a part of moral thinking. Persons can be polluted, desecrated, defiled. If we don't see this, then not only will traditional sexual morality appear opaque to us and inexplicable; we will not be able to develop any alternative sexual morality more suitable (as we might suppose) to the age in which we live.

DESIRE AND POLLUTION

Many features of our present situation provide incidental confirmation of the point. For instance, there is the growing feeling of disgust toward pedophilia. What explains this? Just that the child has not yet reached the "age of consent"? Is child abuse like serving alcohol to a minor? And is that the only reason why we condemn child pornography or wish to keep pornography out of the reach of children (not to speak, though it is now pointless to speak, of everyone else)? Or consider the new sexual crimes, committed often on a campus, where young people believe for whatever reason that consent is what it is all about, the necessary and sufficient condition for "good sex." Sometimes the result is "bad sex"—that sudden sense of violation that ensues when a person recognizes, too late, that consent is after all *not* what it is all about. The result is a charge of "date rape," in itself an unjust assault on the seducer but a last-ditch attempt to make sense of the accuser's own moral feelings. The mess in which many young people find themselves today is proof, it seems to me, that the desacralized morality of the liberal consensus is inadequate to deal with our sexual emotions.

The importance of the idea of pollution can already be seen from the phenomenon of sexual arousal. This is not a state of the body, even though it involves certain bodily changes. It is an awakening of one person to another and a form of communication, in which I-thoughts and you-thoughts are fundamental to the intentionality of what is felt. People look *at* each other, as animals do. But they also look *into* each other and do this in particular when mutually aroused. The look of desire is like a summons, a call to the other self to show itself in the eyes, to weave its own freedom and selfhood into the beam that explores the other. In his incomparable description of the phenomenology of desire Sartre singles out this experience as distinctive of desire and a sign of its metaphysical character—of the fact that it is addressed to the other as a free subject, not as an object.[5] For Sartre the look of desire (*le regard*) summons the

---

[5] Jean-Paul Sartre, *Being and Nothingness*, trans. Hazel Barnes (London: Methuen, 1960), p. 424.

freedom of the other, and he links this feature to the caress of desire, so unlike the caress of affection and yet so nearly indistinguishable, which conjures the other's subjectivity into the surface of the body, there to be revealed and known. The caress and the touch of desire have an *epistemic* character: they are an exploration, not of a body but of a free being in his or her embodiment. But the subject so conjured is at risk. The look that looks into the other might switch to the look that looks *at* the other, so as to assess the body without acknowledging the subject whose body it is. The possibility of pollution and desecration is there in the very phenomenon.

In some such way, it seems to me, we can use the philosophy of the person to reconstruct some of the truths made vivid in the ethic of pollution and taboo: it is what I have tried to do in my book *Sexual Desire*, in which I argue that the phenomena of desire can be understood as parts of a mutual negotiation between free and responsible beings who want each other as persons.[6] As I pointed out in the second chapter, persons are individuals, not just in the weak sense of being substances that can be reidentified and which can undergo change but in the strong sense of being identified, both by themselves and by others, as unique, irreplaceable, *not admitting of substitutes*. This is something that Kant tried to capture in his theory of persons as "ends

[6] Roger Scruton, *Sexual Desire: A Moral Philosophy of the Erotic* (London: Weidenfeld and Nicolson, 1986).

in themselves." Somehow the free being is, in the eyes of all those who are in a personal relation with him or her, the being who he or she is and never replaceable by an equivalent other. In the relations that matter there are no equivalents. Hence there will always be more to sexual morality than the negotiations of free beings under the rule of consent. Their standing as embodied individuals, who cannot be substituted for each other, is what is principally at risk.

PIETY

This brings me to the second objection: that which begins from the situated character of the moral agent, bound by unchosen moral requirements. The concept anciently used in articulating these requirements was that of piety—*pietas*—which, for many Roman thinkers, identified the true core of religious practice and of the religious frame of mind. Piety is a posture of submission and obedience toward authorities that you have never chosen. The obligations of piety, unlike the obligations of contract, do not arise from the consent to be bound by them. They arise from the ontological predicament of the individual.

Filial obligations provide a clear example. I did not consent to be born from and raised by this woman. I have not bound myself to her by a contract, and there is no knowing in advance what my obligation to her at any point might be or what might fulfill it.

The Confucian philosophy places enormous weight on obligations of this kind—obligations of *li*—and regards a person's virtue as measured almost entirely on the scale of piety. The ability to recognize and act upon unchosen obligations indicates a character more deeply imbued with trustworthy feeling than the ability to make deals and bide by them—such is the thought.

Our academic political philosophy has its roots in the Enlightenment, in the conception of citizenship that emerged with the social contract, and in the desire to replace inherited authority with popular choice as the principle of political legitimacy. Not surprisingly it has had little time for piety, which—if acknowledged at all—is confined to the private sphere or to those "conceptions of the good" that Rawls puts to one side in his version of the social contract, since they are the proof that, in their hearts, ordinary people are nothing like the noumenal fictions imagined by Rawls. It would be fair to say, I think, that the main task of political conservatism, as represented by Burke, Maistre, and Hegel, was to put obligations of piety back where they belong, at the center of the picture. And they were right to undertake this task. One thing that is unacceptable in the political philosophies that compete for our endorsement today is their failure to recognize that most of what we are and owe has been acquired without our own consent to it.

In Hegel's *Philosophy of Right*, the family is defined as a sphere of pious obligations, and civil society, as a sphere of free choice and contract.[7] And there is a dialectical opposition between them, with young people naturally struggling against the ties of family in order to launch themselves into the sphere of choice—only to be ensnared by love and the new unchosen bond that comes from it. This dialectical conflict reaches equilibrium for Hegel only because it is *aufgehoben*, transcended and preserved, in a higher form of unchosen obligation—that toward the state, which surrounds and protects all our arrangements, by offering the security and the permanence of law. The bond of allegiance that ties us to the state is again a bond of piety—not dissimilar to that quasi-contract between the living, the unborn, and the dead of which Burke writes so movingly in his answer to Rousseau.[8]

Working out those suggestive ideas in a language that would suit them to the time and place in which we live is not easy. But if it is not done, we will never arrive at a view of political order that grants to it any status more secure than that of a provisional and undefended agreement. To work it out fully we must, I believe, accept the deep insight that Burke, Maistre, and Hegel all share, which is that the destiny of political order and the destiny of the family are connected. Families, and the relationships embraced by them, are nonaccidental features of interpersonal life, just like

[7] G.H.W. Hegel, *Hegel's Philosophy of Right*, trans. and ed. T. M. Knox (Oxford: Clarendon Press, 1952).

[8] Edmund Burke, *Reflections on the Revolution in France* (London, 1790).

the experiences of pollution and violation that I described above.

SACRED AND PROFANE

In all societies rites of passage have a sacramental character. They are episodes in which the dead and the unborn are present. The gods take a consuming interest in these rites, sometimes attending in person. In these moments time stands still; or, rather, they are peculiarly timeless. The passage from one condition to another occurs outside time—as though the participants bathe themselves for a moment in eternity. Almost all religions treat rites of passage in such a way, as "the point of intersection of the timeless with time," to borrow words from T. S. Eliot.

Rituals of birth, marriage, and death are therefore prime examples of the sacred. Such events are "lifted out" of the run of everyday life and "offered up" to the realm of eternal things. Some anthropologists and sociologists have ventured to give explanations of this experience, the best known, perhaps, being René Girard, who traces the experience of the sacred to the sacrificial scapegoating whereby communities rid themselves of their endogenous resentment. Girard's theory, like Nietzsche's theory of morality, is expressed as a genealogy or, rather, a "creation myth": a fanciful description of the origins of human society from which to derive an account of its present structure.[9] And like Nietzsche, Girard sees the primeval condition of society as one of conflict. It is in the effort to resolve this conflict that the experience of the sacred is born.

According to Girard, primitive societies are invaded by "mimetic desire," as rivals struggle to match each other's social and material acquisitions, so heightening antagonism and precipitating the cycle of revenge. The solution is to identify a victim, one marked by fate as "outside" the community and therefore not entitled to vengeance against it, who can be the target of the accumulated bloodlust and who can bring the chain of retribution to an end. Scapegoating is society's way of recreating "difference" and so restoring itself. By uniting against the scapegoat people are released from their rivalries and reconciled. Through death the scapegoat purges society of its accumulated violence. The scapegoat's resulting sanctity is the long-term echo of the awe, relief, and visceral reattachment to the community that was experienced at the death. In Girard's view, we should see a tragedy such as Sophocles's *Oedipus Tyrannus* as a retelling of what was originally a ritual sacrifice, in which the victim is chosen so as to focus and confine the need for violence. Through incest, kingship, or worldly hubris the victim is marked out as the outsider, the one who is not with us and whom we can therefore sacrifice

[9] See René Girard, *Violence and the Sacred* (1972), trans. Patrick Gregory (Baltimore: Johns Hopkins University Press, 1977).

without renewing the cycle of revenge. The victim is thus both sacrificed and sacred, the source of the city's plagues and their cure.

In many of the Old Testament stories we see the ancient Israelites wrestling with this sacrificial urge. The stories of Cain and Abel, of Abraham and Isaac, and of Sodom and Gomorrah are residues of extended conflicts, by which ritual was diverted from the human victim and attached first to animal sacrifices and finally to sacred words. By this process a viable morality emerged from competition and conflict and from the rivalries of sexual predation. Religion, in Girard's view, is not the source of violence but the solution to it—the overcoming of mimetic desire and the transcending of the resentments and jealousies into which human communities are tempted by their competitive dynamic.

The theory is problematic for many reasons, not least because it seems to assume what it is trying to explain—to assume, that is, that the original victim already possesses, in his or her sacrificial state, the aura of sanctity. In this it reproduces the fault exhibited by Nietzsche, in his "genealogy" of morals. Maybe this is a difficulty for all genealogical accounts—either they begin from a state in which the concept is already applied, or they do not succeed in showing how we can come to apply it. Moreover, Girard's theory seems not to encompass the prime example of the sacred as I have described it: the rite of passage in which the community briefly steps aside from time. Those weaknesses apart, the theory bears on those aspects of morality that are germane to the ethic of pollution and taboo. Sacrifice, death, defilement, and miasma—all these are wrapped together in the primeval sense of the sacred, as an intrusion into the world of human freedom from a place beyond. Sacred things are both forbidden (to the uninitiated) and commanded (to those who would live on the true path). They are revealed in "sacraments"—that is, actions that lift their participants to a higher sphere, setting them down among the immortals. Furthermore they can be desecrated and polluted—and this is the most remarkable feature of them. The one who touches the sacred objects without due reverence or in an "uninitiated" state, or who mocks them or spits on them, commits a kind of metaphysical crime. He or she brings what is sacred into the world of everyday things and wipes away its aura. For this people have traditionally suffered the most dreadful of punishments, and the desire to punish remains to this day. Furthermore, Girard puts before us in vivid terms the connection between the sacred and the sacrificial, as well as the importance to both of these of our nature as mortal and incarnate beings. Death is in the background of all sacred objects and emotions, as the thing that they prefigure or the thing that made them what they are.

EVOLUTION AND THE SACRED

Evolutionary psychology will find nothing strange in a view that gives a central place to concepts of pollution, piety, and the sacred in the life of the moral agent. These concepts, and the conceptions that expound them, are easily seen as rationalizations of the "evolutionally stable strategies" of the genes that propel them. And indeed, when it comes to sex and sexual morality, it is remarkable to see how wide is the gulf between what evolutionary psychology would lead us to expect and what liberal morality might acknowledge as legitimate. But I hesitate to rely on evolutionary psychology for the reason that I have already elaborated. A trait is shown to be an "adaptation" just as soon as we can show that its absence will be a genetic disadvantage. In this sense the revulsion against incest is clearly an adaptation. But that says nothing about the *thoughts* on which the revulsion is founded, nothing about the *deep intentionality* of the feelings that it purports to explain. It is therefore entirely neutral concerning their real justification and the ontological ground of the concepts used to express them. An evolutionary psychology of religion will almost certainly show religious belief to be a reproductive advantage, in just the way that mathematical competence is a reproductive advantage (the others have all died out).[10] But evolutionary psychology will leave questions of religious epistemology where they were, just as it leaves the standard of mathematical proof unaltered.

---

[10]See David Sloan Wilson, *Darwin's Cathedral: Evolution, Religion, and the Nature of Society* (Chicago: University of Chicago Press, 2002).

Hence we cannot rely on evolutionary psychology to underpin the concepts and conceptions that I have been considering. Even if we accept the elaborate story told by Girard concerning the origin of the notion of the sacred in scapegoating and ritual violence, this does not *entitle* us to that concept or to the remarkable conceptions that go with it. For sacred things are seen as belonging to *another order* than the order of the empirical world. They are visitors from another sphere: they mark the places in the empirical world from which we look out toward the transcendental. We could *justify* describing them in this way only negatively, by showing the inadequacy of any purely empirical analysis to capture their content while insisting that it is a *genuine* content and one that we clearly understand.

SOME REMARKS ABOUT EVIL

My argument is pushing me toward a difficult position: I want to say both that concepts such as piety, pollution, and the sacred are necessary to us and that their meaning and basis can be derived from the philosophy of the freely choosing person, as I have expounded this. Without transgressing the ontological assumptions of liberal contractarianism, I want to restore the complete picture of the embodied moral agent, as we know this from the literature, art, and religion of our civilization. Other concepts too are involved in filling out the picture, notably the concepts of beauty and of evil. The first of those I have dealt with elsewhere.[11] In lieu of a conclusion to an argument that has opened onto a wide intellectual landscape, I shall make a few remarks about the second of those ideas, ponder its connection with the religious worldview, and leave it to the reader to reflect on how the arguments of this chapter might be incorporated into a believable theory of the person.

We distinguish people who are evil from those who are merely bad. Bad people are like you or me, only worse. They belong in the community, even if they behave badly toward it. We can reason with them, improve them, come to terms with them, and, in the end, accept them. They are made, like us, from "the crooked timber of humanity."[12] But there are evil people who are not like that, since they do not belong in the community, even if residing within its territory. Their bad behavior may be too secret and subversive to be noticeable, and any dialogue with them will be, on their part, a pretense. There is, in them, no scope for improvement, no path to acceptance, and even if we think of them as human, their faults are not of the normal, remediable human variety but have another and more metaphysical origin. They are visitors from

[11] Roger Scruton, *Beauty: A Very Short Introduction* (Oxford: Oxford University Press, 2009).

[12] Immanuel Kant, *Idea for a General History with a Cosmopolitan Purpose* (1784), in *On History*, ed. Lewis White Beck (New York: Bobbs-Merrill, 1964), Thesis 6.

another sphere, incarnations of the Devil. Even their charm—and it is a recognized fact that evil people are often charming—is only further proof of their Otherness. They are, in some sense, the negation of humanity, wholly and unnaturally at ease with the thing that they seek to destroy.

That characterization of evil is summarized in the famous line that Goethe gives to Mephistopheles: "Ich bin der Geist, der stets verneint" [I am the spirit that forever negates]. Whereas the bad person is guided by self-interest, to the point of ignoring or overriding the others who stand in his or her path, the evil person is profoundly interested in others, has almost selfless designs on them. The aim is not to use them, as Faust uses Gretchen, but to rob them of themselves. Mephistopheles hopes to steal and destroy Faust's soul and, en route to that end, to destroy the soul of Gretchen. Nowadays we might use the word *self* instead of *soul*, in order to avoid religious connotations. But this word is only another name for the same metaphysical mystery around which our lives are built—the mystery of the subjective viewpoint. Evil people are not necessarily threats to your body; but they are threats to your self.

We should not be surprised to find, therefore, that evil people are often opaque to us. However lucid their thoughts, however transparent their deeds, their motives are somehow uncanny, inexplicable, even supernatural. Mephistopheles's affability and charm do not disguise the inner torment that he brings with him from the place where he resides. But when it comes to Iago, for example, the villain of Shakespeare's play *Othello*, we are puzzled. We are convinced by him as a character; but our conviction stems from the awe that Iago creates in us. Through his words and deeds Iago prompts the stunned recognition that he really means to destroy Othello, that there is no sufficient motive apart from the desire to do this terrible thing, and that there is no plea or reasoning that could deflect him from his path. After all, Iago seeks to destroy Othello by causing Othello to destroy Desdemona, who has done Iago no wrong. It is the incomprehensible, as it were *noumenal*, nature of Iago's motive that enables him so effectively to conceal it. Peering into Iago's soul we find a void, a nothingness; like Mephistopheles, he is a great negation, a soul composed of antispirit, as a body might be composed of antimatter.

The evil person is like a fracture in our human world, through which we catch glimpses of the void. And here, it seems to me, is one explanation of the phenomenon summed up by Hannah Arendt in the phrase "the banality of evil," which she used to describe what she saw as the bureaucratic mind-set of Adolf Eichmann.[13] The terrible destruction that has been wrought, and deliberately wrought, on human beings in recent times, in the name of this or that political ideology, has not typically been wrought by evil people. As a matter of fact, as Bettina Stangneth

[13] Hannah Arendt, *Eichmann in Jerusalem* (New York: Viking, 1963).

has shown, Eichmann was a pathological hater of Jews and by no means the self-regarding bureaucrat imagined by Arendt.[14] But we can readily assume that Arendt's false description of Eichmann applies truly to other commandants of the concentration camps, many of whom were bureaucrats, given to obeying orders and willing to sacrifice their conscience to their own security when the time to disobey had come. The torture, degradation, and death that it was their role to oversee might not have been, in their own eyes, their doing but, rather, the inevitable effects of a machine that had been set in motion without their help. Evil occurred around them, but it was not something that they did.

Of course, we repudiate the excuses of such people and hold them answerable for the suffering that they might—at a cost—have remedied. We recognize that the death camp was not just a bad thing that happened but an evil that was done. And all the officials were implicated in this evil. As Arendt and Stangneth both point out, the camps were designed not merely to destroy human beings but also to deprive them of their humanity. The inmates were to be treated as things, humiliated, degraded, reduced to a condition of bare, unsupported, and all-consuming need, which would cancel in them the last vestiges of freedom. In other words the goal included that pursued in one way by

[14] See Bettina Stangneth, *Eichmann before Jerusalem: The Unexamined Life of a Mass Murderer* (London: Bodley Head, 2015).

Iago and in another way by Mephistopheles, which was to rob the inmates of their souls. The camps were animated by antispirit, and people caught up in them stumbled around as though burdened by a great negation sign. These antihumans were repulsive and verminous to those permitted to observe them. Hence their extermination could be represented as necessary, and their disappearance into a shared forgetfulness became the spiritual equivalent of matter tumbling into a black hole.

We should not understand the camps, therefore, as dreadful in the way that an earthquake, a forest fire, or a famine is dreadful, even though these natural disasters may produce suffering on just as great a scale. The camps did not exist to produce suffering only; they were designed to eradicate the humanity of their victims. They were ways of using the body to destroy the embodied subject. Once the soul was wiped away, the destruction of the body would not be perceived as murder but, rather, only as a kind of pest control. And I would identify this as a paradigm of evil: namely, the attempt or desire to destroy the soul of another, so that his or her value and meaning are rubbed out. Thus the torturer wishes the will, freedom, conscience, and integrity of the victim to be destroyed by pain, in order to relish the sight of what Sartre tellingly describes as "freedom abjured."[15] In other words, the torturer

---

[15] Jean-Paul Sartre, *L'Etre et le néant* (Paris, 1943), trans. Hazel E. Barnes (London: Methuen, 1957), pp. 393–407.

is using the body to dominate and destroy another's first-person being and delighting in the ruin and humiliation that can be brought about through pain.

I have described the death camps in terms of a purpose. But whose purpose, exactly? This question brings us face-to-face with another of the mysteries of evil, and it is one that has exercised many writers in recent times, from Orwell to Solzhenitsyn. Ask of any individual whether he or she intended the degradation of the death camps, and often it is hard to find an answer. Of course, some of the Nazi leaders, Eichmann included, did intend this, since they were animated by a hatred that demanded the extremes of maltreatment. In the Soviet case, however, the camps continued long after the death of Lenin, Stalin, and their entourage, when nobody existed who had ever intended this result, when possibly even those involved in overseeing the system regretted its existence and when none who made the crucial decisions saw themselves as anything but helpless cogs in the machine.[16]

To say, as many do, that the camps were the work of the Devil is to repeat the problem, not to solve it. For why is it that just *this* metaphor intrudes upon our language when we try to do justice to the facts? The question parallels that of human freedom. From the standpoint of biological science, freedom too may seem like a metaphor: but the concept is forced upon

[16] Anne Applebaum, *Gulag* (London: Penguin, 2010).

us by life itself, as we strive to relate to each other as human beings. It is, in my view, the greatest of Kant's insights to have recognized that we are compelled by the very effort of communication to treat each other not as mere organisms or things but as persons who act freely, who are rationally accountable, and who must be treated as ends in themselves. And even if we think Kant's theory of freedom to be a metaphysical error, there is no denying the phenomenon that it attempts to explain. Likewise we may dismiss this or that theory of evil as fraught with unwarranted metaphysical assumptions. But the phenomenon *itself* is metaphysical—not *of* this world, though *in* it—and this compels us to describe it as we do.

MORALS AND FAITH

The concept of evil, like that of the sacred, describes forces that seem to impinge on our lives from elsewhere. Our understanding of these forces has the same kind of overreaching intentionality that I ascribe to interpersonal reactions. As is implied in the first chapter, there is, in our outlook on the world, an apprehension of the transcendent—a reaching beyond what is given to the inaccessible horizon of the other self.[17] This apprehension informs all our interpersonal

---

[17] I have developed this point in my *The Soul of the World* (Princeton: Princeton University Press, 2014).

dealings; but it also invades our experience as a whole. It is an experience whose ineffability is part of what is valued: for it turns us toward a sphere that cannot be reached by any merely human effort and cannot be known except in this way.

There is a tradition in philosophy, beginning with Plato, that regards the doctrines of divine reward and punishment less as a support for the moral life than as a way of demeaning it. Defenders of this tradition are right to insist that the moral motive is different from the hopes and fears with which religions back it up. Nevertheless, the connection between morality and religion is not an accident, and the considerations raised in this chapter show why that is so. As persons we make ourselves accountable for our actions and states of mind. The very habit of finding reasons that would justify us in others' eyes leads us to demand such reasons of ourselves. Hence even when we are unobserved, we are judged. The awareness of our faults can weigh us down: we seek exoneration and are often remorseful, without knowing the human person to whom an appeal for forgiveness can be made. This is what is meant by original sin, "the crime of existence itself," as Schopenhauer put it—*das Schuld des Daseins*, the fault of *existing as an individual*, in free relations with our kind.[18]

---

[18] Arthur Schopenhauer, *Die Welt als Wille und Vorstellung*, book 3, 51, in *Sämtliche Werke*, ed. Arthur Hübscher (Wiesbaden: Eberhard Brockhaus Verlag, 1940), vol. II, p. 300, writing of tragedy, which concerns the original sin, "die Erbsunde, d.h. die Schuld des Daseins selbst."

Such guilt feelings may be more or less strong. Some people are experts at entertaining them—Al-Ghazālī, for example, Kierkegaard, Novalis. Even in normal people, *hommes moyens sensuels*, these everyday feelings survive the attempt to quiet them. And they prompt the great yearning that finds a voice in tragic art and which engages with our most urgent loves and fears in this world: the yearning for redemption, for the blessing that relieves us of our guilt. Glimpses of this blessing are afforded by such liminal experiences as falling in love, recovering from illness, becoming a parent, and encountering in awe the sublime works of nature. At these moments we stand at the threshold of the transcendental, reaching out to what cannot be attained or known. And that to which we reach, because it promises redemption, must be understood in personal terms. It is the soul of the world, the first-person singular that spoke to Moses from the burning bush.

This reaching for that which is both transcendental and personal engages also with the ethic of pollution and taboo. It animates the distinction between the sacred and the profane. And it gives sense to the ideas of good and evil. The supreme blessing, the forgiveness of the Redeemer, is also a purification, a cleansing of the spirit, and an overcoming of alienation. It is this that we glimpse and reach for in prayer and in those moments when our spirit opens to the sublime. In those moments we accept our being as a gift—it has been *bestowed* on us, and this bestowal is the primary act of creation. And in the encounter with evil we see the opposite of this gift, the negative force that *takes away* what has been given and which focuses especially on the person, the soul, the place where the givenness of being can be most clearly revealed and understood and most spectacularly destroyed.

Those thoughts and experiences represent a kind of deposit in the mind of the moral being—not an explicit theory of the world but a residue of individual existence, which gathers like leaf mold in the forest, feeding the plants that feed it. Religion, seen in this way, is both a product of the moral life and the thing that sustains it. By understanding the world as the gift of a transcendental person, whose real presence is displayed in sacred moments and who cleanses those who pray, we plant our moral thinking in the fertile soil of religious practice. Good and evil, sacred and profane, redemption, purity, and sacrifice all then make sense to us, and we are guided along a path of reconciliation, both to the people around us and to our own destiny as dying things. Even for those who do not consider the dogmas of religion to be literally true, the religious posture, and the rituals that express it, provides another kind of support to the moral life. Religion, on this understanding, is a *dedication* of one's being.

Those thoughts are suggestions only. Rather than burden this short work with my own attempts to explain them, I refer instead to the two great works of art that have attempted to show what redemption means for us, in the world of modern skepticism: Dostoevsky's *Brothers Karamazov* and Wagner's *Parsifal*. In the wake of these two great aesthetic achievements, it seems to me, the perspective of philosophy is of no great significance.

INDEX OF NAMES

INDEX OF SUBJECTS